HORACE'S
SATIRES and
EPISTLES

HORACE'S
SATIRES and
EPISTLES

Translated by
JACOB FUCHS

Introduction by
WILLIAM S. ANDERSON

W · W · NORTON & COMPANY · INC · *New York*

Translation Copyright © 1977 by Jacob Fuchs. Published simultane-
ously in Canada by George J. McLeod Limited, Toronto. Printed in
the United States of America. All Rights Reserved. First Edition.

Library of Congress Cataloging in Publication Data
Horatius Flaccus, Quintus.
   Horace's Satires and Epistles.
   I. Fuchs, Jacob.   II. Horatius Flaccus, Quintus.
Epistolae. English.   1977.   III. Title.   IV. Title:
Satires and Epistles.
PA6396.A2F8   1977   871'.01   77–22300
ISBN 0–393–04479–3
ISBN 0–393–09093–0 pbk.

1 2 3 4 5 6 7 8 9 0

Contents

Preface

A translator must capture the meaning of the work he is translating, the essential, unique quality (including but far exceeding paraphrasable content) that he senses as he reads. I found that I could best translate Horace's meanings by translating his *Satires* and *Epistles* line-for-line, a system quite different from word-for-word, using as my English line one ranging from twelve to seventeen syllables. Preserving Horace's lines, finding again and again an English line to capture the meaning of a Latin line, led to the fashioning of English poems whose meanings I hope translate the meanings of the Latin poems. My method had the additional benefit of forcing me to be concise, to make every word count, as Horace does, and to avoid being overly literal and long-winded in rendering content. I did not hesitate to make exceptions when the necessity of writing readable English required them.

I tried to make my language active and rhythmic and to reproduce the movement of each of Horace's lines, whether the line was all one flow or consisted of several elements balanced against one another. It was important to give the impression of speech, for in the *Satires* and *Epistles* Horace creates a living voice which then creates, for his readers, the man himself. The voice gives life to his moods, his passions, his thoughts, and ultimately to our sense of him as a real person whom we know. I hope that he will come alive for those who read this book.

Horace's many allusions to persons and events offer difficulties of understanding to his modern readers two thousand years later. To ease these difficulties, Mary Hackney has prepared brief footnotes to identify the objects of passing allusions, and a glossary of the more important names that appear more than once in the poems. The glossary is to be found at the end of the book.

This is my place to thank several people who have given me help and encouragement, beginning with Grace O'Connell, who prepared the manuscript. I am grateful to Donald W. Heiney for a good introduction to the art of translation, and to Luci Berkowitz for getting me started as a translator of Horace. More recently, Mary Hackney made her own contribution to my translation. My greatest debt is to William S. Anderson, whose advice was always based on great learning, always delivered with great tact.

For My Brother

Introduction

The works translated in this volume constitute slightly more than half the total poetic output of Horace. The *Satires* are the work of the young poet; the *Epistles* were produced by a middle-aged man who at least says that he feels age creeping up on him and limiting his choices. It is only to be expected that the themes of the *Epistles* and the tone of the poet-speaker should differ from those of the *Satires*. However, with all the differences, there is a remarkable constancy in these two separate works, and readers regularly group them together. Both deal mainly with moral topics from an informal and practical point of view, trying to work on the ethical sense of the individual and thereby to improve his attitudes and behavior. Both employ a similar poetic form, a form which Horace had inherited for the *Satires* and decided to continue in the later *Epistles*. As one encounters echoes and variations of earlier themes in the *Epistles*, as one compares the older person with the younger writer of the *Satires*, a fuller and richer impression is gained of the sensitive, dedicated ethical intelligence that most readers over the centuries have admired.

Horace did not come lightly to his convincing attitude of moral seriousness. Born in 65 B.C., two years before the future ruler Augustus, he experienced directly and indirectly the conflicts, anxieties, losses, and successes of the next thirty-five years, with seemingly few opportunities given him by birth to emerge from their political, social, and economic chaos into that world of rational unconcern which surprisingly characterizes him when we first encounter him in the *Satires*. If we knew Horace only from the *Satires*, we never would have been able to reconstruct the troubled years he had experienced as a young man. What he does tell us about his previous life is limited, to *Satires* 4 and 6 of Book I, and in both instances he introduces us to selected aspects of his father. His wonderful father *(pater optimus)*, he declares in 1.4.105 ff., used to give him homespun lessons in ethics, which were calculated to correct the faulty behavior and thoughts of young Horace. Thus, it was Horace Senior who implanted in his son the proclivity to study practical morality, principally so that he could improve himself, rather than to humiliate others by publishing their faults. Having presented his father in 1.4 as the justification for his satiric method, Horace in 1.6 in a different fashion reintroduces the old man, who had died, it appears, some time after the murder of Caesar in 44 B.C. when the younger Horace was away in Athens; and this time he surprises us by concentrating on the fact that Horace Senior was born a slave and only later received his freedom. That humble, not to say base, background, which his enemies repeatedly bring up with sneers, Horace not only freely admits but actually turns into a reason for legitimate boasting. His "wonderful" father deserved that adjective not because he came from a noble family and passed on to his son all the great aristocratic political heritage we regularly hear about in a Scipio or Metellus, for example; nor did he come from a well-established, wealthy equestrian family, as Cicero did, able to use the family business and social connections to maintain prosperity and develop a solid political base. Born of an ex-slave, Horace had little chance of succeeding in the manner most highly regarded in Rome, through politics. Instead of protesting against his bad luck, though, or even lying about his birth, Horace professes to be grateful to his ex-slave father for giving him a liberated attitude about the best goals in life, for freeing him from the burdens of political ambition for the true pleasures of poetry and ethical study.

It is evident that these two different but related pictures of the father, wonderful not in spite of but even because of his slave background, have been chosen by Horace to support important motifs of the *Satires*, not to give us all the necessary biographical data by which to reconstruct a full picture of Horace's formative years. We come away from 1.4 and 6 knowing what Horace wants us to know about some basic reasons for his special satiric methods and his professed indifference to the temptations of political machination.

Have we any other sources for data that would enable us to elaborate, perhaps qualify this heartwarming picture of father and son? There are incidental reflections of Horace's childhood in his native town of Venusia in Apulia. For example, in *Satire* 1.6.71 ff., we hear that, though he was a poor owner of a barren little field, the father refused to allow his boy to go to school with the hulking sons of gigantic ex-centurions. Such schoolmates would have lowered the quality of local education, and Horace's father wanted his son to have the best, on a par with the sons of Roman senators. At great personal cost, then, he moved from Venusia to the capital. But Horace did not forget some of the natural beauty of the Apulian countryside; references to it often creep into his lyric *Odes*, and those first experiences in a rural setting no doubt determined his lifelong preference for country living, not as a poor man in a barren little field but as a comfortable owner of a modest piece of property and seven or eight slaves to maintain it.

What it was like to live in Venusia when the political tensions of the 50's were bringing the people of Italy to a ruinous Civil War; what it was like to be in Rome in 49 or 48 B.C. as Caesar decided that war was inevitable and then, in surprisingly swift moves, drove Pompey out of Italy, chased him over to Greece, and forced him to the decisive engagement at Pharsalia: this, Horace never tells us. Shortly after Caesar's victory, young Horace had completed his Roman education, and his self-sacrificing father scraped up the money to send him over to Athens for the equivalent of a university experience. Of that exciting sojourn abroad, Horace gives us a glimpse in *Epistle* 2.2.41 ff. He was immersed, he says, in the moral lessons of the Academy when war broke out again and tore him away from that happy place. What Horace refers to is a new phase of civil conflict that began after the murder of Caesar in March 44. Brutus, one of the murderers, failed to consolidate his position in Italy and fled to Greece in search of military backing. An able speaker and a "hero" of the young idealistic Romans in Athens, he swept Horace and others off their feet to risk all for the cause of Liberty. So Horace fought on Brutus' side at Philippi in 42, in that desperate battle where Octavian muddled through to victory while Brutus and Cassius died. Defeated or, as Horace puts it, "with clipped wings," he gave up and returned to Italy to face a dubious future. With his father apparently dead and the modest estate lost or confiscated, Horace regarded himself as a poor man. It was in these unpromising circumstances that he began to "make verses," as he deprecatingly declares.

The *Satires* of Book I, along with some of the *Epodes*, are the earliest surviving verse that Horace produced. These ten *Satires* were completed before Horace was thirty. During those years, Horace held a position as a government clerk, and all the poems reflect the experience of one who lives in Rome. He tells us especially in *Satires* 5, 6, and 9 of his close association with Maecenas, the trusted and powerful friend of Octavian, who managed the city while Octavian was absent on necessary campaigns. Despite the invidious comments of outsiders, Horace insists that his association with Maecenas is nonpolitical; it owes its origins to his poetic talents and the efforts of Vergil to introduce him to a worthy patron. As he describes his manner of dealing with Maecenas and his otherwise simple life, Horace modestly presents himself as a model for contented existence in an otherwise highly troubled time. For the most part, he adopts an Epicurean outlook: he rejects avarice as painful (*Satire* 1); he warns against adultery as bringing more trouble than pleasure (*Satire* 2); he espouses reasonable friendship (*Satire* 3); he shows his indifference to politics (*Satire* 5); and points out its burdensome elements (*Satire* 6); he pokes fun at those who get excited over silly rivalries (*Satire* 7); by means of a cowardly Priapus he ridicules certain superstitions (*Satire* 8); and he desperately defends the integrity of Maecenas' apolitical friendship (*Satire* 9). The Horace that speaks in the *Satires* has assumed the character of a wise Epicurean, far removed from the wild political struggles to which he had so recently committed himself in Greece.

What precisely is this satire that Horace has chosen as his first topic of verse? He answers that question to some extent in two *Satires* of Book I, in lines to which I so far have made no reference, *Satires* 4 and 10. In *Satire* 4, using the image of his father, he describes a type of poetry that is partly traditional but modified by both an Epicurean sense of responsibility and an insistence on artistic control which comes from the "new poets" of Catullus' generation. A clever and sharp-tongued poet named Lucilius had invented poetic satire about a hundred years earlier and had stamped upon the genre the associations which it continues to carry even today in our dictionaries: e.g., "the use of ridicule, sarcasm, irony to attack vices, follies, etc." Notice the belligerent verb "attack" and the mainly cruel devices of ridicule and sarcasm; such satire does not instruct, does not present a reasonable ideal such as that of the Epicurean. It is Horace's great contribution to present a difficult, but viable, alternative to the Lucilian brand of caustic satire: he aims not to attack vice but to reason with people whose faults can be corrected, who can be brought into the Epicurean world of rational pleasure away from the basically painful goals that have tempted them. Unlike Lucilius, he does not score off easy targets of folly, does not call attention to his own cleverness: his satire is conditioned by the moral constraints of his father's training and his later adopted Epicureanism and by his dedication to poetic restraint (*Satire* 10). So, to use a phrase from *Satire* 1, he tells the truth with a smile, as a good friend should.

In Book I, the urban satirist speaks in a moderate but definitely didactic manner, with an assurance and apparent wisdom which ought to surprise us in one so young, so recently a participant in a flawed political cause. Not long after the publication of these ten *Satires*, Maecenas gave Horace a present which affected his life style from then on: he made him the owner of a small rural estate in the Sabine Hills, where Horace could escape the hustle and bustle of Rome and recapture some of the natural beauty he had known in his youth. During the next four or five years, while Octavian and Antony were steadily growing farther apart and finally facing each other in the decisive battle at Actium, Horace worked on the eight poems that would form Book II of the *Satires*. Both because of the personal independence symbolized in the Sabine Farm and because of his own poetic development, Horace made some key changes of approach in Book II. We now no longer listen to the moderate but clear teachings of the contented Epicurean; the prevailing tactic of these eight new *Satires* is to force exaggerated instruction on us from a motley variety of self-assured, but mostly wrong-headed, personalities: a lawyer, Trebatius, confidently telling Horace how to write poetry (*Satire* 1); an austere and untutored rustic Ofellus shrilly advocating the most unpalatable of simple foods (*Satire* 2); a wild Damasippus interminably arguing that everyone but himself (including Horace) is insane (*Satire* 3); a fanatic Catius reciting from memory some gourmet teachings which he wrongly conceives as the way to achieve true Epicurean happiness (*Satire* 4); a mock-heroic Tiresias who anachronistically teaches an un-heroic Ulysses how to recoup his financial losses by insinuating himself into the wills of childless millionaires (*Satire* 5); an absurd slave Davus who preaches to Horace, his master, the paradox that all people are "slaves" except the wise man—and Horace is not wise (*Satire* 7); and a host Nasidienus who ruins his meal and his guests' enjoyment by reciting all his gourmet lore to them (*Satire* 8). Only in *Satire* 6 do we hear the voice of Horace for any appreciable time, a Horace who now expresses his contentment with country living. However, even in *Satire* 6, Horace yields the floor at the end to a somewhat pompous Cervius, who preceeds to "teach" us through the fable of the diminutive country and city mice. There was nothing quite like this method of presentation in the tradition before Horace; it suggests his increasing personal diffidence, his greater confidence in his audience, his pleasure in an indirect and almost "comic" method of satiric teaching.

Between the *Satires*, completed just after Actium in 30 B.C., and the first book of the *Epistles*, completed in 20 B.C., the Roman world witnessed the optimistic beginning of the Augustan Era, and Horace himself published his masterpiece, a collection of *Odes* in which his basically ethical interests adopt a lyric manner. Perhaps not entirely content with the reception of these *Odes*—probably, too, finding the lyric manner less congenial at the age of forty than the informal conversational tactic he had developed in the *Satires*—Horace openly announced at the beginning of his next poems, the *Epistles*, that he was giving up the unseasonable lightness of lyric and devoting himself to moral study, trying to fashion an ethical existence which could satisfy him as he grew older.

Of course, there is something disingenuous about such a statement, for, while studying to live rightly, Horace is also writing very careful poetry about the process and using the fictional persona of the letter writer to communicate with his public. He is poet and moralist to the end. The epistolary strategy allows him considerable freedom. Generally, he appears to us urbane, modestly self-ironic, but morally concerned; yet, thanks to the intimate conventions of letter writing, he does not preach or teach so much as to talk to younger people in an avuncular manner or to his equals in an urbane but serious tone. It is important to sense the adjustment of the letter to the purported addressee: it is also often important to see how the separate locations of Horace and his addressee fit into the themes of the poem. For example, he devises quite different messages for the travelers Florus (*Epistle* 3), Celsus (*Epistle* 8), and Bullatius (*Epistle* 11). At other times, clearly locating himself on his Sabine Farm, he develops his discussion around various tensions between the city and the country (*Epistles* 7, 10, 14, 16, 17, 18). Like ordinary letters, the *Epistles* regularly start from a particular dramatic situation, interested questions about the addressee, brief comments on Horace's activities and whereabouts, but then they plunge, as few letters do, through the surface of friendly trivia to the ethical meanings that can be extracted from any set of activities. Horace presents himself with even less assurance than in Book II of the *Satires*, as a neophyte, an eclectic who can or will follow no philosophic school consistently, a kind of late beginner committed to finding his ethical way, but by no means claiming that he yet possesses any other truth than that it is high time for him and others to get serious. A number of the letters consider Horace's achievements and vocation as poet (*Epistles* 13, 19, and 20) as well as the literary inclinations of others (*Epistle* 3), and they confirm his commitment, declared in *Epistle* 1, to abandon playful verse (and some of his youthful ambitions for poetic glory that led him to write it) in order to devote himself totally to truth and the moral life. From now on, then, his poetry must subserve that ethical pursuit.

During the following years, as he left his forties behind and entered his fifties, Horace published one more book of fifteen substantial *Odes*, wrote a lengthy lyric poem to honor a patriotic celebration not unlike our own Bicentennial, and in three long *Epistles* busied himself with the public and private roles of the poet in Augustan Rome. Those three literary *Epistles* close this collection on a challenging note. The earliest of these may well be *Epistle* 2.2; it is addressed to the same Florus he had previously written in 1.3, and deals at greater length with the familiar theme of subordinating verse-making to ethical concern. The other two, first the so-called *Art of Poetry* (*Ars Poetica*) and then the letter to Augustus (*Epistle* 2.1), focus on the public responsibilities of the poet and on the chief patron of poetry in Rome, Augustus himself. They are not easy discussions, for the obvious reason that writing good poetry, as Horace knows and insists, is no game for children. Thus, the *Art of Poetry* turns out to be anything but the expected polished performance. After offering some easily remembered rules, Horace bears down on the underlying principles that should control poetry, the need to refine and shape the first emotional surges of "inspiration." The insane poet, unable to restrain his impetuous feelings and disordered verse, is compared by Horace with the "mad" philosopher Empedocles who, according to popular myth, ended his life by jumping into the fiery crater of Mt. Etna; this is the very role which Horace has rejected for himself. As he wrote in *Epistle* 2.2, he struggles with clear-eyed sanity to understand life and to write forcefully about it. The poet's public "art" and private "life are two aspects of a single personal existence. The other side of the coin is analyzed in *Epistle* 2.1, namely, the responsibilities of Augustus as patron of literature. Ostensibly explaining why he himself is unworthy of patronage as a writer of humble conversational verse rather than epic panegyric, Horace lays out some important critical ideas about poetry that implicitly justify his own methods as well as those of the obviously admirable epic poets Vergil and Varius. It is the job of the patron to discern true quality in poetry, not merely to agree with popular prejudices and to reward hoary stereotypes. From the ideal patron, what Horace modestly calls his conversational pieces that crawl along the ground will earn the highest esteem.

It cannot be said that these final three *Epistles* make much use of the epistolary fiction. Because of their slight dramatic occasion and their vast length, they seem more like essays. However, the persona of Horace, what I earlier called the "sensitive, dedicated ethical intelligence," encounters us here as before. He who said, in his early *Satires*, that he criticized others only to instruct himself and improve his character, has shown in these final literary essays his mature sense of ethical responsibility, as he has probed the very depths of the craft which has occupied all of his attention ever since he crept home "with clipped wings" from defeat at Philippi.

William S. Anderson

The Satires

Book I

1

Why is it, Maecenas,[1] that no one, no matter what role
he's chosen for himself or what his fate offers him,
lives with it in peace, but envies the lives of other men?
"Those sailors have it easy," says the old soldier,
burdened by his years, broken down by hard campaigns.   5
But the sailor says, as the south wind rattles his boat,
"The army's better. Why? You fight: in an hour's time
either death comes quickly or victory that makes you glad."
Someone who knows all the statutes and laws envies farmers
when, at cockcrow, his client comes rapping on his door.   10
A farmer, dragged to town because he'd put up bail and had to come,
loudly announces that folks are happy living nowhere else.
There are other examples, so many that even gabby Fabius
would get tired of telling them. Not to delay you more,
here's my point. Suppose a god appeared and said, "Hello!   15
I'm here to make you anything you want. You, the soldier,
be a sailor; and you, the legal expert, be a farmer.
Stop playing your old parts, there's been a change. Well?
Why don't you move?" They wouldn't, they'd reject true happiness.
How could Jupiter not get so angry, with good reason,   20
that he'd puff out his cheecks and swear that never again
would he offer such a receptive ear to mortals' prayers?
I have more to say, but I'll skip the usual comic patter.
But tell me what law is violated if someone laughs
while speaking truth? You know how teachers sometimes give   25
their pupils little cakes, to help them learn their ABC's.
But I won't fool around; this is a serious discussion.
The farmer breaking up hard soil with a plow,
the cheating innkeeper, the soldier, the brave sailors
who race over every sea all know why they sustain   30
their toils: to retire when old, to relax and be secure,
for then they'll have assembled enough provisions. Look at
the tiny ant (they'll tell you) who works hard and drags in
by mouth all that goes into the store she gathers;
she thinks about the future and prepares for it.   35
But as soon as January shades the cycling year,
the ant stops crawling out and enjoys whatever she has.
She has good sense. But a raging storm wouldn't make you
cleave less to money. Nor would winter, fire, the sea, and swords.
Nothing would even slow you, if another man had more money.   40
How does it help a fearful soul like you to be cunning

1. See Glossary for this and all proper names of importance not identified in footnotes.

1

and hide an immense weight of gold and silver in the earth?
"But if you nibbled at it, you'd end up with one lousy cent."
But if you don't, what's the value of such a high-piled heap?
A hundred thousand bushels may be threshed upon your floor,   45
that won't make your belly hold any more than mine. If you
were in a slave-train and made to haul the bread bag
on your weary back, you'd get no more than the slaves
who carried nothing. Look, how can it matter to a man
living within nature's limits if he plows a hundred acres   50
or a thousand? "It's nice to draw from such a big reserve."
When from my little heap I can take as much—you'll grant that—
why do you praise your granaries over my grain bins?
As if you wanted a drink, no more than a pitcher full
or glassful and said, "I'd rather drink the same amount   55
from a big river than from this little stream." And so,
those who enjoy quantity more than they really should
are ripped away with roaring Aufidus's banks and carried off.
But a man who only asks for what he needs will drink
no mud-fouled water, and he won't lose his life by drowning.   60
Still, since false desires fool a large portion of mankind,
they'll tell you, "Nothing's enough. What we own, we are."
What can you say? Say, "Be miserable," for that's the choice
they freely made. They're like an Athenian I heard about
Rich and stingy, he thought nothing of the people's snide remarks,   65
and always said, "They hiss me, but I applaud myself
at home, as soon as I lay eyes on the money in my chest."
Tantalus is thirsty and gapes for water as it flees
his lips . . . what's so funny? Change the name and it's you
that myth's about. You have money bags amassed from everywhere,   70
just to sleep and gasp upon. To you they're sacred,
or they're works of art, to be enjoyed only with the eyes.
Don't you know the value of money, what it's used for?
It buys bread, vegetables, a pint of wine and whatever else
a human being needs to survive and not to suffer.   75
Staying awake half-dead with terror, living night and day
in fear of ogreish thieves, of fires, of slaves who might
rob you as they run away—you like this life? Of such
advantages I hope I'll always be thoroughly deprived.
"But if a chill is waging war upon your health   80
or if other illness has driven you to bed, you have someone
to sit close, apply dressings, and ask the doctor to come
so you'll be cured, restored to your heirs and loving family."
Your wife doesn't want you cured, neither does your son; all
your friends and neighbors hate you, every boy and girl.   85
Are you surprised, when before all else you put money,
that no one will offer you love, which you didn't earn?
Nature gave you a family, you didn't have to work for it.
But now if you wanted to get and keep their friendship
you'd be wasting your time, I must tell you, like a man   90
who tried to get his ass to race without a whip.

In short, let your getting end; and, because you have more,
fear poverty less. You might begin to work a little less,
since you've got what you desired, and not be like Ummidius.
His story isn't a long one: he was so extremely rich   95
he needed to measure his money, so stingy his clothes
were no better than a slave's. Until the final minute
of his life he was obsessed by one fear in particular,
of running short of food. But a freedwoman, Tyndareus's
fiercest daughter,[2] split him down the middle with an axe.   100
"What are you suggesting? That I should live like Naevius
or Nomentanus?" Why match such opposed contestants
in the same ring? No, though I forbid you to be a miser,
I'm not ordering you to become a wastrel or a bum.
Rupture and castration are a long distance apart.   105
There is a mean in living, there are fixed boundary lines,
and the good can't support itself outside of them.
Now I return to where I started, that no miser
likes himself. Instead, he envies the lives of other men
and, if someone else's goat should drag a bigger udder,   110
he wastes away. He won't compare himself to most people,
so always as he hurries someone richer blocks his way.
When horses pull their chariots from the starting gate
a driver will go after those outracing his, despise those   115
he overtakes; they all might as well be running last.
That's why we rarely find anyone who admits he's led
a happy life and is prepared to leave it, pleased
with the time he spent, like a guest after a good dinner.
Well, enough. Since you might start thinking I've robbed   120
the bookshelves of sore-eyed Crispinus, I'll stop talking.

2

The ecdysiasts' local, the affiliated quacks,
the touts, tramp actresses, comedians—this whole tribe
is gloomy and worried since Tigellius the singer died.
"What a generous man." But another man fears the name
of prodigal and won't give his poor friend any help   5
when he could keep the cold away and banish hunger's bite.
And another, asked what crazy impulse makes him waste
a fine inherited estate to serve his own ungrateful gut,
buying with borrowed money every kind of gourmet treat,
answers that he doesn't want to be considered cheap and mean.   10
By some citizens he's praised, condemned by others.
Fufidius fears a reputation as a wastrel or a bum,
though rich in land, rich in cash he loans at interest;
his quintuple cut he slices from the principal in advance,
and as his debtor nears collapse he rides him harder.   15
He hunts for customers who've just put on a man's toga,
boys with strict fathers. Who wouldn't shout, "Some deal!"

2. The freedwoman is compared to the legendary Clytemnestra, daughter of Tyndareus, who murdered her husband King Agamemnon with an axe.

after hearing this? And add, "He certainly must live well
with all that money." Well, amazing as it seems,
he's not even his own friend, and the father in Terence   20
who led such a wretched life after driving out his son
wasn't any harder on himself than was Fufidius.
By now you may be asking, "What's your point?" It's this:
Veering away from one vice, fools collide with its contrary.
Malthinus walks around with his skirts drooping; another,   25
a model of style, wears his hoisted to his rotten crotch.
Rufillus smells like candy, Gargonius like a goat.
No middle ground. Some men won't touch anything but skirts
whose borders hit the floor and hide the heels of wives,
others nothing not for sale inside a smelly brothel.   30
Seeing a man he knew come out of such a place, Cato
praised him—"Decent fellow!"—and spoke wisely as a god:
"When lowly lust has swollen up their veins, young men
do right in coming here instead of grinding wives
not theirs." "That commendation," says Cupiennius, "I'll   35
decline"—admirer that he is of white and wifely cunt.
It'll pay to listen to me if you don't like adulterers
to have fun and do like them to suffer through and through,
to get no pleasure that isn't marred by enormous pain
and comes rarely anyway, almost never without lots of risks.   40
One of them dived right off a roof, another was beaten
until he died. Another fled into the clutches of a gang
of hard-assed hoods. One guy ransomed his skin with cash,
one was raped by stableboys, and there was also a case
wherein a pair of balls and hungry prick were cut off   45
with a sword. "Quite right too," all say, except for Galba.
But the second class stuff isn't necessarily safer,
freedwomen I mean, over whom Sallustius goes crazy,
no less so than the stud who chases wives. But if moved
as good sense and economy direct, to temper munificence   50
with moderation, as he should, a man desired to be both
generous and right, he'd give what is enough, not unseemly
and a waste. But on one point some men hug themselves
and love and admire themselves. "I don't touch married women."
So Marsaeus once said, Origo's admirer, who gave   55
that starlet his ancestral fortune and his land.
"Never for me," he said, "any funny stuff with wives."
But funny stuff with mimes, and with whores too, injures
your good name more than it does your wallet. Is it enough
not to go around seducing wives if you hurt yourself   60
some other way? A reputation lost, your inheritance
wiped out: bad business no matter how you do it. What's
the difference who ruins you, a wife or a serving girl?
Villius, dubbed Sulla's son-in-law,[1] wretchedly deceived

---

1. Refers to a scandal before Horace's time. Fausta, the
aristocratic daughter of Sulla, was married to Milo but
had other lovers. Among them were Longarenus and

Villius, derisively called the "son-in-law" because of
the frequency of his visits.

by Fausta's noble name, was punished enough and more   65
than enough, pummeled with fists and struck at with a sword,
excluded from the house while Longarenus was inside.
Now suppose, speaking for the prick, who saw the whole mess,
Villius's mind had asked their owner, "What do you want? Did I
ever ask you for a fancy cunt, born to a great consul,   70
swathed in a long dress, even when I was at my hottest?"
What would he have answered? "The girl has a famous father."
But nature, who has a special store of riches, will guide you
better and in quite another way, if only you would choose
to be a wiser manager and not confuse desirable goods   75
with those you should avoid. Maybe it's your fault you suffer,
maybe fortune's; don't you think it makes a difference?
Rather than be sorry, stop chasing wives; all that gets you
is trouble, a belly full, from the fruits you try to pluck.
A great lady with jewels glinting green and pearly white   80
will rarely have a thigh more smooth (yes, Cerinthus) or calf
more shapely than a hooker; that's usually the way it is.
And also, she displays the goods without pretense, plainly
showing what's for sale, not—if one part is really good—
thrusting that out to be observed, concealing all the others.   85
Rich men have a trick when buying a horse: they inspect
it covered up, so if it looks good but has tender feet,
as horses often do, a wavering buyer won't be sold
by a beautiful hind end, neat head, or powerful neck.
That's the right way. Don't study, Lynceus-eyed,   90
a body's good points, then be blinder than Hypsaea
to its flaws. Those legs, those arms! But she's thin-assed,
big-nosed, skinny in the hips and too long in the feet.
With wives you can't judge any feature but the face;
all the rest, unless it's Catia, the long dress hides.   95
If what you're after is denied you by defenses
and therefore drives you wild, you have a real problem.
Attendants, litter bearers, hairdressers, hangers-on
the dress down to the heels, the wrap that covers all,
everything gets in the way, and you just can't see her.   100
With the other, no problems. Almost naked in her Coan gauze,
she allows you easily to check for ugly legs or feet.
You can measure her figure by eye. Or do you prefer
being fooled and parted from your money before you get
to see the goods? A lover sings about a hunter who "trails   105
a hare through deepest snow, ignores her when she rests,"
and then explains: "My passion's just the same; it too
flies past prey available to all, chases prey that flees."
With this slight song do you expect to banish pains
and fevers from your heart and throw off your weight of trouble?   110
Ask nature what boundary she sets to passion, what she needs
for herself, what, if denied, hurts her—these questions
are useful. So is, "How do truth and appearance differ?"
When thirst is burning in your throat, must you have gold cups?

When you're hungry do you despise all foods but peacock   115
and turbot? So when your member swells, if you have
a serving girl convenient, or serving boy, to satisfy
the impulse on the spot, why endure a prick about to blow?
Not me. It's the available I like and getting an easy lay.
Mrs. "wait a minute," "more money," "when Hubby leaves"   120
give to the eunuch priests, says Philodemus; he takes
a girl who's fairly cheap and comes when called for.
If she's pretty and well shaped and clean, not caring
to be any taller or any whiter than nature designed,
then, when her left thigh lies beneath my right she's my   125
Ilia and Egeria, any name I like. And I don't worry,
while we fuck, about a husband come back from his farm,
doors broken down, dogs howling, an enormous commotion
shaking all the house, the ghost-white wife jumping
out of bed, the maid screaming, already fearing the blows,   130
the wife afraid that she'll be poor, myself afraid for me.
So, barefoot, with my tunic flapping open, I must flee
to save my money, or ass, or, above all things, my name.
It's bad to be caught. Let Fabius be judge, I'd convince him.

← caught at adultery

3

All singers have this failing: when they're with friends
they can never persuade themselves to sing when asked;
unasked, they'll never quit. That's how that Sardinian,
Tigellius, was. Octavian could have ordered him to sing,
but asking him as a friend, and as his father's friend,   5
wouldn't have worked. In a musical mood, he'd bellow
choruses of "Hello, Bacchus" from first course to last,
droning the low notes and shrieking after the high ones.
He was extreme in everything. Often he ran as if pursued
by enemies, more often marched like a maiden bearer   10
of Juno's sacred gifts. Sometimes he owned two hundred slaves,
sometimes ten. One moment he'd babble about kings and despots,
the next he'd say, "Just give me a three-legged table,[1]
a plain shaker for unscented salt, and any rag of a toga
to keep me warm." Suppose you gave this simple soul,   15
so undemanding, one million sesterces.[2] Within five days
he wouldn't have one left. He used to stay awake all night
till morning and snore all day. There never was a man
so out of order. Someone might now ask me, "And you, don't you
have faults?" Yes, but others, and maybe not so bad.   20
Maenius was bitching at Novius behind his back when asked,
"Are you perfect? Or, as if we didn't know you, are you
trying to make us think so?" "I'm an exception," he said.
This is stupid, brazen self-love, and I condemn it.
Since your vision blurs when you look inside yourself,   25

---

1. An elegant dinner table was supported by a pedestal.
2. Under the empire the as and its double, the dupon-
dius, were the most common monetary denominations;
the sesterce, minted of brass, was equal in value to four
asses. Thus, a million sesterces comprised a considerable sum of money.

why study your friends' bad qualities with eyes as sharp
as an eagle's or snake's? The favor will be returned,
and your friends go searching for the ugly things in you.
"He's kind of touchy, and he doesn't really smell right,
not to a sophisticated nose. You have to laugh at him,   30
that hayseed haircut, that baggy toga, those shoes
hanging loosely on his feet." But he's a fine man,
the best, but he's your friend, but he has great talent
hidden underneath his sloppy hide. Anyway, shake yourself
to see whether nature planted your vices in you   35
or, perhaps, your own bad habits did, for it's certain
that in neglected fields grow weeds that must be burned.
You can make exceptions, you know. A lover fails to see
his girl's bad features; sometimes he even likes them,
as Balbinus liked the sight of Hagna's tumorous nose.   40
I wish we made the same sort of error with our friends,
and that our moral standards had given it a decent name.
We should favor our friends as a father favors his son,
and not despise them for their faults. If a boy's a squinter,
his father calls him Wink. Little Bird is a pet name   45
for a runt, like that famous old dwarf, Sisyphus.
A kid with bent legs is called Stumpy. And if the son
totters on weak pins, the father beams at little Wobbles.
A man's too cheap; say he's economical. Another is loud,
and he's socially crude; he only wants his friends   50
to think he's funny. Another argues, too ready to say
whatever's on his mind. Call him honest and open.
Someone has a hot temper? Spirited, you mean. I'm sure
this way of thinking can both make and keep men friends.
But we turn a man's very virtues upside down   55
and love gumming up a clean decanter. To anyone among us
who lives quietly and decently we give mocking names,
Chicken and Creep. Another keeps away from every trap
and never shows his unprotected side to any evil:
he understands the world and knows that bitter envy   60
and libel do well in it. We call someone as wise as this,
someone who won't take chances, a shifty, crafty fake.
But a man can be too direct (like me when I happily burst in,
Maecenas, on you) and bother someone who may be reading
or enjoying some quiet, just to talk. "Pushy bastard,"   65
we say. "He doesn't have an ounce of simple tact." Yes,
how foolishly we pass an unjust law, against ourselves.
For none of us is born without some faults; the best man
only bears the lightest load. A good friend is a fair one
and weighs my virtues against my weaknesses to see   70
(I hope the virtues win) which I have more of. He will,
if he wants my friendship: I'll weigh him on the same scale.
If you don't want your wens to nauseate your friend,
you'd better forgive him for his warts. It's only right
that if pardon is asked for faults, it must be given too.   75

Moreover, since anger can't be wholly rooted out,
nor any other failings that inhere in fools, why not
use reason to weigh offenses so that each of them
is punished in proportion to its status as a crime?
Suppose a slave, ordered to take away a plate, 80
had dared to taste the bits of fish and cooling sauce;
if he were nailed to the cross for that, sane men would call
his owner madder than Labeo. How much greater and madder
a mistake is this: A friend has done some little thing,
and not to forget it will make you look sullen and mean. 85
But you hate and avoid him as if he were Ruso and you
a debtor around the fearful first, forced to get
the interest or principal from somewhere or hear
his awful histories, like a captive waiting for the knife.
A drunken friend peed on the couch or from the table swept 90
a little plate Evander's hands wore smooth. For this,
or because he took the chicken from my part of the plate
when in a hungry mood, is he any less my friend,
my valuable friend? What would I do if he'd stolen something,
or broken his promise, or refused to honor his bond? 95
Those who say all crimes are equal[3] don't face reality.
Human feelings and customs oppose this idea; so does
the general good, the mother of justice, or close to it.
When living creatures crawled out upon the primal earth,
a mute and ugly herd, they battled over dens and acorns 100
with fingernails and fists, then with clubs, and finally
with real weapons, which in time their need provided.
At last they discovered language, and it shaped their voices,
expressed their feelings. They stopped making constant war
and began to build cities; they made laws against theft 105
and violence and also against the crime of adultery.
For earlier than Helen cunt was the most shameful cause
of war, though we have no record of those who died
after taking, as beasts do, the females that they wanted;
a stronger man killed them, the bull of the herd. 110
Fear created law. That's the truth, as you must admit;
just take a look at the history of all the world.
Nature doesn't know right from wrong, as it knows
pleasure from pain, dangers from desirable things.
And philosophy can't prove it's the same and equally wrong 115
to break off young cabbages in another man's field
as to make nocturnal thefts of sacred relics. So, use
a scale which assigns penalties according to the crime
rather than scourge someone who only needs a whipping.
Let me add that my worry isn't that you'll spank a man 120
who should be beaten, not if you count pilfering as equal
to piracy and would threaten both great and small offenders

3. The Paradoxes of the school of Stoic philosophers were precepts which, though they seemed to contradict everyday experience, were believed to state fundamental truths. One of these stated that all crimes were equally deserving of blame; in *pro Murena* 29. 60 ff., Cicero gives as an illustration the equal culpability of a man who needlessly strangles a rooster and one who strangles his own father.

with the identical scythe "if only men allowed me
to be king."[4] But if the wise man is also wealthy,
a good cobbler, the only really handsome man, and a king,   125
why do you want to be what you already are? "You don't
understand Papa Chrysippus. A wise man doesn't make
his shoes or sandals, but a wise man is a cobbler." Why?
"Well, suppose Hermogenes is being quiet; he's still
a singer, the very best. Skillful Alfenus, having thrown out   130
all the tools he once employed and closed his shop,
is still a cobbler. Therefore, the wise man is best,
the very best at every trade, therefore a king." Street boys
like to pull your beard. If you don't keep swinging
with your staff, they'll push you and plague you until,   135
Greatest of Great Kings, you crack up and start to scream.
I'll be brief. You can pay royal visits to the baths,
the penny ones, and have one follower in your train,
that idiot Crispinus. But I have good friends
whom I can trust to forgive me if I stupidly screw up,   140
just as I'll gladly forgive any failings in them.
King, as a mere citizen I live more happily than you.

4

Eupolis, Cratinus, Aristophanes—those poets,
and the others who shared in creating Old Comedy,[1]
would expose anyone who deserved it—a slimy thief,
an adulterer, a killer, someone made notorious
for other crimes—by showing him plainly on the stage.   5
On these writers Lucilius wholly hangs; he followed them,
changing only the feet and numbers. He was sarcastic,
with a sharp and haughty nose, but he wrote clumsy verse.
This was his mistake: often in an hour he'd compose
two hundred lines, a stunt, like standing on his head.   10
His stream's muddy flow holds things we'd happily remove.
He chattered, too lazy for the labor of writing,
of good writing; quantity I don't care about. Here's
Crispinus, glad to give long odds: "Get your paper.
Bring it and I'll bring mine. Let's appoint judge, place,   15
and time, and then find out who piles up more lines."
The gods deserve my thanks for making me so weak and timid,
the type who speaks rarely and then not very much.
Go ahead, you, stuff yourself with air like a bellows
and blow away until the fire makes the iron soft;   20
that's what you like. Fannius, that happy man, unasked
sets up his shelves and busts, but my stuff no one reads.
I'm afraid to recite in public,[2] with good reason:
people don't much like my kind of writing, for most of them

4. The Stoics believed that only the sage was perfect,
since only he lived in harmony with Reason and Nature.
Therefore, according to Cicero's formulation of the
Paradox in *pro Murena* 29. 61, only the wise are beautiful, rich, and kings among men.

1. Comedies produced in Athens during the fifth cen-

tury B.C. Its most prominent playwrights were Eupolis,
Cratinus, and Aristophanes, though only eleven plays
of Aristophanes remain today. The plots of Old Comedy
are fantastic, but in their course prominent contem-
poraries are often parodied and ridiculed.

2. Public recitations were common in Rome.

may be rightfully accused. Pick anyone out of a crowd,   25
you'll find you get a victim of avarice or ambition.
One man is mad for screwing wives, another boys.
Silver has made a slave of one; Albius is stunned by bronze.
The trader buys and sells from the sun's rising place
to the land its setting warms; through catastrophes   30
he's hurled, like dust caught in a storm, afraid to lose
any part of what he has, or afraid it won't get bigger.
Every one of these men fears poetry and hates poets.
"Mad bulls! Run, get far away! They like to raise
a laugh and won't spare anyone, including friends.   35
Whatever they smear on their pages they want the world
to know, even the slaves and old women coming home
from the public pools and ovens." And now, a brief rebuttal.
In the first place, I don't count myself among those
I consider poets; it's a mistake to think that putting words   40
in meter is the only thing they do, or that anyone
like me—my things are more like conversations—is a poet.
Reserve for men with genius, with inspiration, with grand
and resonating voices, the distinction of that name.
That's why some men have asked whether or not comedy   45
is poetry: it lacks strength as well as noble feeling
in both language and subject. It differs from talk in having
a fixed foot; otherwise, talk is all it is. "No passion?
The father raves at his spendthrift son who loves his whore
and won't accept a bride bringing a big dowry with her,   50
who gets drunk—what a disgrace!—staggering around
the town before it's dark." But would Pomponius hear
a milder speech if his father were alive? You see,
it's not enough to write lines composed of words so common
that any father might well say them, if you broke the meter up,   55
not just the actor father. Take the pieces I write now,
which Lucilius used to write. If you disarranged the feet
and rhythms, and made the first word within a line its last,
the present last its first, the result would be different
than if you mangled in the same way "After Discord foul   60
had burst battle's iron gates and iron doors asunder."[3]
There you'd still see poetry, even in the severed pieces.
Well, another time I'll consider whether I write poems.
My question now is, should you really be so apprehensive
about this kind of writing? The informers, shrewd Sulcius   65
and Caprius, carry notebooks and make their croaking rounds.
Robbers are frightened of either one, but any good man
whose life and hands are clean can safely scorn them.
And though you may resemble Caelius and Birrius, the robbers,
I'm not like Caprius or Sulcius. Why be afraid of me?   70
Not a single bookstore or stand displays my little books
for anyone to put his sweaty hands on, even Hermogenes.

---

3. A quote from Ennius' epic poem, the *Annales*. The imagery and choice of words in this passage are full of poetic suggestion, and remain so even when the word order is altered.

I recite only to my friends, when they insist on it,
not wherever I am and before anyone. Many poets
read their work in the center of the Forum and the baths,   75
where the enclosed voice makes charming echoes. The fools,
they like that and never wonder if they're being boors
or if they've picked a bad time. "You like to inflict pain,"
you say, "you mean to, and it's cruel." What informant
supplied you with this charge to hurl? Was it anybody   80
I know, who knows me? "A man who bites at absent backs
and won't defend a friend against a charge that he's gone wrong,
who hungers for men's loud laughter and the reputation of a wit,
who can invent what he didn't see but can't keep secrets
to himself—that man has a black soul. Roman, beware!"   85
At a dinner where three couches hold four diners each,
often you'll see one guest throwing dirt on all the others,
though not the host; but after wine he smears him too,
when truthful Liber opens hearts and shows their contents.
What a funny guy he is, the life of the party, to you,   90
hater of black souls. But if I laugh because ridiculous
"Rufillus smells like candy, Gargonius like a goat,"[4]
why do I strike you as spiteful and mean? If mention
were made before you of Capitolinus' supposed thefts,
you would defend him like this, in your usual style.   95
"Capitolinus has been to me both benefactor and friend
since my boyhood, and many things I wanted done, when asked,
he did. I'm delighted that he's safe and can stay in Rome.
But still, I just don't see how he ever won acquittal
at the trial." This is black as squid's ink, this is   100
pure corruption. It will never be found on my pages,
or in my heart before I write. If I can promise anything,
I promise that. No, if I express myself too freely,
if perhaps I laugh too much at people, grant me my right
and your indulgence. The best of fathers made me this way.   105
By the use of bad examples he taught me how to live.
When urging me to lead a simple, sober kind of life
and be content with what he could provide, he would say,
"You know, don't you, that young Albius lives in poverty
and that Baius is broke? That's what happens to a son   110
who wastes his father's money." If he didn't want me entangled
with some slut, he might say, "Avoid Scetanus's mistake,"
and if I had eyes for someone's wife, with legal sex around,
I would hear, "Trebonius was caught, he won a foul name."
He used to tell me: "A philosopher could give you theory   115
on what you should avoid or seek. For me it's quite enough
to maintain the standards that our ancestors passed down,
and keep your life and reputation safe while you need me
for a guardian. When manhood comes to make you strong
in mind and body, you'll swim without a float." These words   120
my father used to shape me, always giving examples

---

4. Quoted from Horace's own *S.* 1.2.27.

whether he urged an action—"Do what he did," he'd say,
and mention one of the special jurymen—or forbade one:
"This thing you're planning will only hurt and shame you.
How can you doubt this? You know about that dirty talk   125
boiling around X and Y." Death next door makes gluttons ill,
scares them, and the death-fear gives them self-restraint.
Just so, when someone else is shamed, often young minds
will fear to make that man's mistake. Raised as I was,
the ruinous vices don't bother me, only middling ones,   130
which I hope you'll excuse. I may grow nearly free
even of these with the help of time, an honest friend,
or my own advice. For whether reading on my couch
or walking on the street, I don't neglect myself. "That's good."
"That would improve my life." "My friends would be happy   135
if I were like that." "Not pretty what he did. Could I,
not thinking, do the same?" I keep after myself like this,
though not a word of it leaves my lips. In my leisure time
I play with paper. That's one of those middling sins, only
one of them, and if you won't pardon me for practicing it   140
the army of poets will arrive in strength, reinforcements
to back me up (we outnumber everyone else) and, just like
the Jews, we'll force you to convert and join our mob.

5

Rome's grandeur left behind, I was met in Aricia[1]
with moderate hospitality. Heliodorus the rhetorician,
most learned of Greeks, came with me. Then, off to Forum Appi,
full of boatmen and crooked innkeepers. We were lazy
and spent two days getting there. Those with quicker legs   5
do it in one. The Appian Way is easier if you go slowly.
Here, since the water was unspeakably bad, I declared war
upon my stomach, waiting in sour spirits for the others
in the party to finish eating. Now Night brought darkness
forth upon the earth and prepared to flood heaven with stars.   10
Now shout followed shout, slaves to boatmen and boatmen
to slaves: "Land here!" "Don't overload us, dammit!" "Enough,
we're packed!" Settling the money and hitching up the mule
waste at least an hour. The horrible gnats and swamp forgs
forbid all sleep. Drunk on cheap wine, the boatman sings   15
about his girl back home. A passenger joins in to make
a contest. Eventually he gets tired and goes to sleep,
so the lazy boatman lets the mule feed itself its dinner,
tying its rope around a stone, and then flops down and snores.
Come daybreak and we see that our boat isn't moving at all;   20
but finally someone with a temper pounces on the mule

1. Horace relates his overland journey to Brundisium (38 or 37 B.C.) as part of the entourage of Maecenas, who was then traveling to represent Octavian at a summit conference to reconcile his differences with Marc Antony. Maecenas was accompanied by Fonteius Capito, a close friend and representative of Antony, and Cocceius, who was probably to serve as arbitrator. Maecenas' own entourage, whom he joined at Anxur, included several literary friends—Horace himself, Vergil, Plotius Tucca, Varius, and the Greek rhetorician Heliodorus. All these people are mentioned in the poem. Horace traveled a distance of about 340 miles in two weeks and passed through the places he names, beginning with Aricia.

and on the boatman, whacking away at skulls and butts
with a willow rod. By midmorning we've barely made port.
We wash our hands and faces, Feronia, in your waters.
After breakfast, we creep along three miles, climbing   25
white rocks—visible, gleaming, far away—to high Anxur.
Here we're to meet Maecenas and the distinguished
Cocceius, both authorized to speak in great affairs
of state, both skilled at solving problems between friends.
And here I get an inflammation and have to smear my eyes   30
with black salve. Soon Maecenas arrives, and also
Cocceius. Fonteius Capito comes then too, a man
with no flaw in him anywhere, and Antony's best friend.
Fundi, in the magistracy of Aufidius Luscus, we leave
with joy, laughing at the crazed ex-clerk and his prizes,
the purple-bordered robe, striped tunic, pan of coals.²   35
In the Mamurrae's hometown, exhausted, we rest a while,
Murena supplying us a place to live, Capito a kitchen.
The next morning's sun rises most happily for me, since
Plotius and Varius meet us at Sinuessa, and Vergil
is there with them. Nobler souls than these never dwelled   40
on earth, and no one has closer ties to them than I.
O what embraces we shared, and what great rejoicing!
Nothing compares, I think, when thinking right, to a good friend.
Near the Campanian bridge a government hostel shelters us,
and the officers in charge give us supplies.   45
Then, at Capua, the mules put their saddles down early.
Maecenas goes to play games, Vergil and I go to sleep;
ball throwing doesn't amuse the red-eyed and sour-stomached.
We stay at Cocceius's well-stocked farm, north of Caudium
and its inns. At this point that little sharp-talking leech   50
Sarmentus had a fight with Messius Cockadoodle, of which,
Muse, I would hear, beginning with the parentage of those
who met in war. Messius is of noble Oscan blood³;
Sarmentus's line goes back to his owner. Thus their lineage.
And now the battle: First Sarmentus. "A wild horse, that's you,   55
a real snorting stallion." We laugh. Messius doesn't mind.
"Damn right," he says, and jerks his head. "And if your brow
still had its horn uncut," Sarmentus adds, "you'd be a terror;
even with it cut, you're quite a fright." For an ugly scar   60
disfigured his forehead on the left, beneath its bristles.
Campanian rot, jokes Sarmentus, and goes on about his face.
Then he asks him to perform Cyclops' shepherd dance:
with those looks he'd need no tragic mask or heavy boots.
Now Cockadoodle has a lot to say. Would Sarmentus give   65
his slave chain to the lares?⁴ And though now a clerk,

---

2. Aufidius, though probably merely an aedile, displays his senatorial pretensions by wearing the official dress of a praetor. The pan of live coals is carried with him for burning incense in honor of Maecenas' arrival.
3. Horace recites in mock-epic style the genealogies of the two "combatants." The Oscans were regarded by the Romans as proverbially oafish; a slave was regarded, legally, as having no family at all.
4. A slave who had escaped slavery, possibly by running away, might dedicate his chain to the lares (see Glossary) as an offering.

didn't his old mistress own him just the same? He ends
by asking why he ever fled: for he could fill himself
upon a pound of corn a day, he was that skinny and small.
That's the kind of dinner we like, and we take our time.   70
Then we go straight to Beneventum, where a diligent host
nearly burns his place down while cooking bony thrushes.
For through his old kitchen a vagrant flame veered,
from a fallen volcano of logs, mounting high to lick the roof.
Hungry guests, terrified slaves snatch the food to safety,   75
everyone tries to put the fire out—quite a scene.
From here on, Apulia starts to display some mountains
familiar to me, those the sirocco parches, and which
we would never have crawled over if near Trevicum
a farm hadn't given us a reception, including teary smoke   80
from wet branches and leaves smoldering in the fire.
Here, utter moron that I am, I lie awake till midnight
waiting for a liar of a girl who never came. Sleep takes me
in the middle of a fantasy and my dreams are so real
that I make a mess on my clothes and on my belly.   85
Then we're whisked twenty-four miles by carriage
to stay in a village whose name won't fit into meter,
so I offer an obvious hint: the most common of things
must be bought here—water. But its bread is the best,
and wise travelers usually bring some along for future use.   90
For in Canusium it's gritty, and they don't have any water
there either, in that town brave Diomedes founded long ago.
Here Varius leaves us, which makes all his friends upset.
From there we move on to Rubi, tired when we arrive,
having gone rather far on a road that was all mud.   95
The weather improves next day, but the footing is worse
right up to fishy Barium's walls. Then Gnatia, built
while water spirits sulked,[5] gives us good reason to laugh:
they try to tell us incense melts upon their temple's steps
without fire. Apella the Jew may believe this if he likes,   100
not I; I've learned about the tranquil life the gods enjoy
and know, whatever miracle nature makes, the gods
won't give up their peace to send it down from heaven.
At Brundisium the long trip is over; now this long page is too.

6

Maecenas, none of the Lydians who settled
in Etruria[1] were nobler than your ancestors,
and both your grandfathers once had huge armies
under their command. But you do not, as many do,
turn up your nose at men of obscure origin,   5
men who are like me, a freedman father's son.
Since you show no interest in the parentage of anyone,
of anyone born free, you seem to be convinced

---

5. Gnatia, like the unnamed village mentioned in lines
86–89, was short of water.

1. Maecenas' forebears belonged to the ancient Etruscan aristocracy, traditionally believed to be the descen-
dants of colonists from Lydia, in Asia Minor.

that even before humble Tullius was king,
there were many men with nobodies for ancestors   10
who lived exemplary lives and won high offices.
On the other hand, though Laevinus was descended
from Valerius, who drove proud Tarquin from the land,
he was worth about as much as a penny. Even the people
saw that, and you know how brainless they can be,   15
often electing worthless men and being stupid slaves to fame.
They're stupefied by titles and by masks.[2] And how should
we behave at our far, very far, distance from the crowd?
For the people could have put Laevinus into office,
not Decius the newcomer, and I might have been purged   20
from the Senate by Appius, for having no freeborn father.
But I'd have deserved it, for not staying silent in my own skin.
Behind her glittering chariot Glory draws in chains
both highborn and low. Tillius, what did you gain
in getting your lost stripe[3] back and becoming a tribune?   25
Envy of you mounted; it bothers plain men less.
The instant that some maniac wraps black thongs
around his calf[4] and draws the stripe across his chest
he promptly hears, "Who is he, and who was his father?"
If someone had the same sickness Barrus had, a craving   30
to be considered cute, no matter where he went
the girls would study all his features one by one,
eyeing his face and calves, his hair, feet, and teeth.
And when someone vows to guard the city and the people,
to protect the Empire and Italy and maintain the temples,   35
his father's rank, his mother's origin (it may be low)
concern us all, and what these are we all must learn.
"You, a son of Syrus or Dama or Dionysius,[5] you would dare
to execute Romans yourself, or send them to the cross?"
"But my colleague in office, Novius, sits behind me,   40
he's now what my father was." This makes you a Paulus
or Messalla? Besides, Novius has volume. In the Forum,
when two hundred wagons tangle with three big funerals,
he shouts over trumpets and horns. At least we notice him.
Now I come back to myself, a freedman father's son,   45
whose back everybody bites, as a freedman father's son.
Now because my life, Maecenas, twines with yours, once
because a Roman legion obeyed me as their tribune.
These charges differ: though I might be envied an office
that I held, friendship's not the same, especially yours;   50
you offer it only to those you think deserving,
men free of warped ambitions. I don't think "lucky"
well describes me. I didn't become your friend by chance.
Nothing accidental made me yours. First Vergil,

---

2. Waxen masks of the ancestors, with inscriptions
beneath them listing the offices each had held, were
hung in the atrium of a family's house as proof of the
family's antiquity and nobility.
3. The distinctive mark of senatorial rank was a broad
purple stripe on the tunic. Tillius had been expelled
from the senate but later had regained his position.
4. Senators wore a shoe with such thongs.
5. Common names for slaves.

best of men, and then Varius told you who I was.   55
When I met you I stuttered and I could barely talk.
I was bashful and nothing I said came out right.
But I didn't tell you I had a famous father or land
near Tarentum on which I liked to ride my nag.
What I am, I make evident. Your answer, as usual,   60
is very brief. I go. Nine months later you recall me
and place me among your friends. I hold it a great honor
to have pleased you: you judge a man's worth or foulness
by considering his life and morals, not his father's fame.
But if my faults aren't many and aren't major,   65
and my character is generally a decent one, rather like
a handsome body spotted with an occasional mole,
if no one can justly blame me for being cheap, or low
in my habits and pleasures, if I'm pure and unspoiled
(I don't mind admitting it), and if all my friends like me,   70
the reason is my father, poor possessor of a tiny farm.
He wouldn't send me to Flavius's school with its huge boys,
from huge centurions sprung, who carried their slates
and schoolbags slung over their left shoulders and paid
eight cents tuition on the fifteenth of every month.   75
Instead, he dared to take me off to Rome, to learn
the liberal arts that senators and knights have taught
to their sons. If anyone in the bustling city
noticed my clothes and retinue of slaves, he surely
thought I'd paid for them out of my own ancestral wealth.   80
My father was himself my guardian, inflexibly moral,
near me among my teachers. Why say more? I stayed clean;
all virtue starts with that. He kept me free of every vice,
not only in my actions, but in my reputation too.
He wasn't afraid of looking like a fool someday   85
if as an auctioneer or tax collector, like himself,
I made low wages. And I wouldn't have complained. But,
as things are, I owe him greater praise and greater thanks.
Nothing can shame me, while I'm sane, in such a father.
Nor will I say, as many would, that I can't be blamed   90
just because my parents weren't freeborn or famous.
That's not my defense, it's a way of thinking and speaking
far distant from mine. If a law of nature had us start
our lives again, after we'd reached a certain age, allowing
us to indulge our self-esteem by picking out our parents,   95
I'd be happy with those I had before, not some new ones
honored by the fasces and curule chair.[6] "Insane," the crowd
would tell me (you, perhaps, would think me sane), but
I'm not used to such a heavy load and wouldn't want it.
Because right away I'd have to go looking for more money,   100
and have visitors at home and attendants when I travel,

6. The insignia of Roman magistrates. The fasces, or rods, honored praetors and consuls; the ivory curule chair (its name deriving from the word for chariot) distinguished curule aediles and censors. These offices, along with the quaestorship, were held in order of increasing importance: quaestor, praetor, consul, censor. The aedileship was not a regular part of this *cursus honorum*.

so that I'd never be alone either out in the country
or abroad. I'd have to feed a mob of horses and grooms
and take wagons everywhere I went. Now, a small mule
is enough to take me to Tarentum, if I like,   105
although his back might blister beneath me and my gear.
No one would call me stingy; not so you, Praetor Tillius,
when you travel to Tibur followed by a mere five slaves,
carrying with them a wine hamper and a chamber pot.
Here, noble Senator, my life is easier than yours,   110
and in a thousand other ways. Wherever I wish, I go,
alone. I ask how much the grain and produce cost,
often wander in the sharpies' circus[7] and the Forum
after hours. I watch the fortune tellers, then go home
and eat my dinner of leeks, peas, and plain pastry.   115
It's served by three boys, and on my white stone table
stand two cups and a dipper; there's also a flask,
a cheap one, and for my oil a simple jug and saucer.
Then I go to sleep with no gloom about rising early
next morning to go and visit Marsyas,[8] he who   120
hates the sight of the younger Novius's face.
In bed till ten, then I take a walk. Or, after reading
or writing something I may like, in private, have a rub,
and not with the oil dirty Natta stole from the lamps.
When I get tired and the sun, grown hotter, reminds me   125
of the baths, I flee the Campus and three-cornered catch.
After lunch, not a big meal, enough so that I don't pass
the day with my belly empty, I stay around the house.
This is my life, free of worrisome, painful ambition.
I enjoy knowing that I live more agreeably than if   130
my grandfather, father, and uncle had all been quaestors.[9]

7

How proscribed Rupilius Rex, full of pus and poison,
was punished by Persius the half-breed is, I believe,
known to all barbers and to every case of inflamed eyes.
This Persius was rich, had huge transactions cooking
at Clazomenae, also irksome legal quarrels with Rex.   5
He was tough and could outdo Rex at throwing mud,
a cocky blow-hard so pungent in his patter
that, up against Barrus and Sisenna, he'd be favored.
Back to Rex. When nothing could be done to make
the two agree (and surely every pair of pests has   10
the same privilege as heroes locked in combat. Between
Hector, Priam's bold-spirited son, and Achilles burned
a mortal anger, and death alone could finally part them;
they quarreled only because each had so much courage,
no one more. If there's bad feeling between cowards   15

7. The Circus Maximus, where swindlers gathered.
8. An attendant of Bacchus, traditionally represented with a wineskin on his left shoulder and his right hand raised. His statue stood in the Forum, and Horace implies that its upraised arm expresses abhorrence at the looks of the younger Novius, a usurer whose stall was nearby.
9. A rather ironic remark, since the quaestorship was the lowest magistracy on the *cursus honorum*.

or if unequal fighters meet in battle, like Diomedes
and Glaucus the Lycian, the less eager man will run
and send presents too), during Brutus's tenure as praetor
in rich Asia, Rupilius and Persius squared off, no less
an even match than Bithus and Bacchius. Into court   20
the heroes charge, each of them magnificent to see.
Persius unfolds his case, is laughed at by everyone,
the whole gathering; he praises Brutus and his retinue.
Brutus he calls the "sun of Asia," "propitious stars"
is his title for the retinue, except for Rex, the "dog star"   25
that farmers hate. Persius rushed on like a river
newly thawed in a region far too wild for the axe.
Then the Praenestine met this great and salty flow,
firing back in purest vineyardese, like a picker
in the fields who's tough and won't back down an inch,   30
as passers-by admit, though they call him crazy as a loon.
But Greek Persius, deluged with Italian vinegar,
shouts out, "By the great gods, Brutus, I beg you.
You're used to making kings extinct[1]: why not butcher
this one? I'm serious! Here's a chance to show your stuff."   35

8

Once I was a fig tree's trunk, a piece of useless wood.
Then a craftsman, unsure whether to make Priapus or a bench,
decided on the god. So I'm a god, to thieves and birds
a terrifying sight, for my right hand threatens thieves,
as does the red rod thrusting from my ill-bred crotch.   5
For the meddling birds I have a reed upon my head
to scare them and keep them out of these new gardens.[1]
Once the bodies of the poor came here, after removal
from their tiny rooms, in boxes bought by fellow slaves.
This was the common grave for all the low and wretched,   10
for Pantolabus the leech, Nomentanus the spendthrift.
"A thousand feet across, three hundred deep," the pillar read,
and also: "This cemetery plot doesn't go to the heirs."
Now men live happily on the healthful Esquiline and
go walking on the sunlit wall from which sad faces   15
used to overlook a field made hideous by whitening bones.
But I have to worry, and not just about the thieves
and beasts that are a customary menace here;
worse are those who work with magic spells and potions
on men's souls. There's no way I can drive these witches out,   20
or, once the wandering moon shows all her lovely face,
stop them from gathering bones and harmful plants.
I saw, I myself saw, in her hoisted black dress walking,
Canidia, her feet bare, hair hanging free, howling like mad;

---

1. Persius puns on the name of his adversary Rupilius
Rex, since *rex* in Latin means "king." A Brutus had
driven out Tarquinius Superbus, the last king of Rome,
in 509 B.C., and the Brutus of this poem had helped to
assassinate Julius Caesar, the dictator of Rome.

1. This plot of land on the Esquiline Hill, now being
converted by Maecenas into personal gardens, had formerly been a burial ground. Thus in *S.*II.6.32–33
Horace refers to the "dreary . . . Esquiline" where he
goes to meet Maecenas.

Sagana was with her, an older witch. Their pale faces 25
made them dreadful sights. Then they gouged at the earth,
using their nails, and they bit a black lamb into chunks.
The bloody streams were mingled in a ditch to summon up
the dead, spirits who knew how to answer questions.
They had a wax doll and a larger, woolen one; this they 30
placed above the wax figure as if to show who ruled;
the little one lay there groveling, like a slave
about to die. One witch invoked Hecate, the other
cruel Tisiphone. That was your chance to see serpents,
and hellhounds, and the blushing of the moon, who hid 35
behind the mightly tombs rather than witness what went on.
If I'm lying about this, may white crowshit fall on me,
and may I be both pissed and crapped on when visited
by Julius, frail Pediatia, and Voranus the thief.
Why give the details? The way the speaking shades responded 40
to Sagana, taking turns, all the while buzzing shrill and sad,
how those sly and secret witches buried a wolf's beard,
and a snake's tooth, then threw the wax doll in the fire
to make it blaze, and how I (an audience soon to be avenged)
shuddered at those two Furies' voices and their deeds. 45
Then, loud as a pig's bladder when it bursts, I farted,
as my figwood buttock cracked, and they hightailed to town,
Canidia dropping her teeth, Sagana her towering wig;
along with these they also lost their plants and magic bracelets.
It was a crazy, funny scene. You'd have really laughed. 50

9

I was walking on the Sacred Way, thinking, as usual,
about some little poem that had me totally absorbed,
when someone rushed up—his name was all I knew of him—
and snatched my hand, saying, "Old friend, how are you!"
"All right, for now," I said. "And I hope you're doing well." 5
When he followed, I spoke first, "Need something?" He said:
"Yes, your acquaintance. I'm clever—worth knowing." I said,
"How impressive." Pathetically, I tried to get away,
walking fast, stopping short, whispering urgent nonsense
into the ear of the boy with me, the sweat dribbling down 10
upon my heels. "Bolanus,[1] my friend, you're lucky *your* temper
is short." So I thought to myself. He babbled away,
praised the streets, the city. I didn't answer him,
not a word. "You're just dying to get away," he said.
"I know. Well, forget it. I'm sticking right with you. 15
I'll come along wherever you go." "No reason you
should come. I've got to see someone you don't know,
way across the Tiber by Caesar's Gardens, and very sick."
"I'm not busy, and I'm not lazy. Take off, I'll follow."
My ears droop and I give in, like a donkey who's resentful 20

---

1. Horace thinks enviously of his hot-tempered friend, who would not for long have allowed a sense of courtesy to mask his real feelings.

when too much is loaded on his back. Then the sales talk:
"I know my character, and I tell you: don't prefer Viscus
as a friend, or Varius, for who can write more poems
than I, or write them faster? Who more lightly moves his limbs?
And Hermogenes would get quite jealous every time I sing."   25
That was my chance for cutting in: "Do you have a mother,
or relatives who rely on your good health?" "Nobody,
I've laid them all to rest." They're lucky. I'm left,
so finish the job. Now I meet my sorry fate, foretold
when I was young by the old Sabellian with her urn[2]:   30
"No dreadful poison will finish him off, no hostile sword;
neither pleurisy, nor a cough, nor a lingering case of gout.
Someday a jabbering fool will be his ruin. Big talkers,
if he would be wise, he'll run from as his years advance."
When we arrived at Vesta's temple, half the morning   35
was already gone, and he was supposed to be in court,
if he weren't there he'd lose his case. "For friendship's sake,"
he says, "come and help me out a bit." "May I drop dead
if I'm of use in courts or know anything about the law.
And I'm rushing, you know where." "I'm undecided," he replies.   40
"Should I drop my suit or you?" "Me, me!" He answers, "Nope,"
and proceeds to stride ahead. Since it's hard to fight
one's conqueror, I must follow. "How does Maecenas treat you?"
he asks. "The man has a very sound mind and very few friends.
No one has used good fortune better." "I'll work for you,   45
I can be a great second player and take the minor roles;
just make some contacts for me, that's all. I'll bet my life
you'll outdo everyone you know." "We don't live that way,
the way you think; there's no house more honest than his,
none more resistant to bad feeling. I don't care, you see,   50
if someone has more money or learning. There's a rightful place
for each of us." "Quite a story. And quite hard to believe."
"But it's true." "Now I'm even hotter to get near him."
"Your desire is all that's necessary: To a hero like you
he'll fall in a flash; he's an easy man to conquer,   55
so he makes first penetrations difficult." "I'm confident.
I'll bribe his servants. And if today, for example, I'm
repulsed, I won't quit. I'll find a chance, bump into him
in public, walk places with him; without great labor
life gives us mortals naught." And so on. But suddenly I see,   60
and in our way, Aristius Fuscus, who grasps this character's
character in an instant. We chat. "Where've you been?
Where're you going?" The usual. So I begin to pluck,
to pull, at his thick arms, nodding my head at him,
blinking my eyes for swift salvation. He plays with me,   65
smiles and acts innocent. My liver tingles with rage.
"Surely you said you wanted to tell me something,
something confidential?" "Oh, yes, but I'll choose
a better time. Today is the thirtieth Sabbath. Why offend
the circumcised Jews?" "I don't care about religion," I moan.   70

2. From which she drew or shook out inscribed lots which she then interpreted.

"But I do. I'm a bit more of a conformist, just one of many.
So please excuse me. See you later." Ah, that a sun
so black should rise over me! The traitor flees, leaving me
beneath the blade. But then fortune brings his legal foe.
"You crook," he yells, "where do you think you're going?"   75
And then, "Sir, will you testify?" So I offer him my ear.[3]
He carries my companion off to court. Shouting on both sides,
confusion on all sides. That's how Apollo preserved me.[4]

10

Yes, I said it[1]: Lucilius wrote lines that run on clumsy feet.
What supporter of Lucilius is so stubborn as to disagree?
Yet this same satirist, because he scoured the city
with large quantities of salt, was praised on the same page.
I'll grant him that, but not everything else; for then   5
I'd have to admire the farces of Laberius as lovely poems.
After all, to pull a gaping grin out of your reader
won't suffice, though there's virtue even in that.
The work must be concise, so that thoughts unfolding
aren't tangled up in words that weigh down tired ears.   10
The language should be grave at times, but often funny,
sometimes rhetorical and poetic, sometimes urbanely smooth,
an easy flow with its strengths restrained and purposely
toned down. Frequently a clever stroke is better,
abler in cutting at big problems than something serious.   15
Our forerunners, the men who wrote the Old Comedy,
were masters at this and should be our models, but cute
Hermogenes never reads them, and Monkeyface down there
hasn't learned to chant anything but Calvus and Catullus.
"But Lucilius did so much by mixing Greek and Latin   20
in one poem." Oh, you finally noticed! You think that
such a hard, amazing trick? Even Pitholeon of Rhodes
could handle that. "But a style blended out of both languages
is nicer, like Falernian wine when you mix some Chian in."
Only when composing verse, I ask you, or also when   25
you have the tough assignment of Petillius' defense?
Would you then forget father and fatherland (the Latin
of lawyer Poplicola, by the way, he carefully prepares,
as does Corvinus), and mix into our native language
words borrowed from abroad, in the bilingual, Canusian style?   30
I too, an Italian born, once planned to write in Greek
some little poems, but Quirinus came and told me not to
(and I saw him after midnight, the time of truthful dreams):
"Bringing wood into a forest is no crazier than this,
your plan to join the crowded squadrons of the Greeks."   35
While the Inflated Alp[2] keeps pumping, and murders Memnon,

---

3. According to ancient custom, Horace assents to act
as a witness by allowing the litigant to touch his ear.
4. Apollo, as the patron god of poetry and poets, looks
after Horace. The phrasing here is a parody of the *Iliad*
20.443, where Apollo rescues Hector.

1. Refers to Horace's previous criticisms of Lucilius
(see Glossary) in *S.I.4.8–12*.

2. A sarcastic nickname for the poet M. Furius
Bibaculus, who wrote epics on the Gallic Wars and on
the Ethiopian king Memnon, slain by Achilles during
the Trojan War. His bombastic style is parodied also in
S.II.5.40–41.

misshapes the muddy head of Rhine, I enjoy my own things,
which won't be heard in the temple where Tarpa judges
or return over and over for performance on the stage.
The clever courtesan, Davus, and Chremes, their old dupe,   40
chatter away in plays that only you, of living men,
Fundanius, with your casual air, can write. Kings' deeds
are for Pollio to chant in triple-beating verse[3]; the epic,
with its strength, Varius can best compose. Grace and sweetness
are Vergil's gifts, from the Muses who love the countryside.   45
Satire remained, at which Varro Atacinus tried and failed,
he and others. I could write it better than those people,
worse than its inventor[4]; from his head I'd never dare remove
the crown which fits so well and brings him so much praise.
But I did say his was a very muddy stream and often bore   50
more worth taking out than keeping. Tell me, Professor,
in great Homer is there nothing you can carp about?
Did casual Lucilius want no changes in the tragedies
of Accius, never laugh at Ennius's less majestic lines?
Yet he never claimed to be better than those he criticized.   55
After reading Lucilius, why aren't we allowed to ask
whether it was his own coarseness or his subject matter
that kept his verse from being more precise and moving
with more grace? Perhaps his skill at knocking out hexameters
pleased him so much he loved to write two hundred lines   60
before he ate, and just as many afterwards. Cassius
Etruscus had that same talent, he flowed more quickly
than a rushing stream, and they say his books and shelves
were made into his pyre. Lucilius was, I don't deny,
casual and witty, and he wrote with more technique   65
than some raw beginner in a form untouched by Greeks,
and than the poetic rabble of his time. But even so,
had fate allowed his life to reach down to the present day,
he'd file his work down very fine and cut out all
that was excess. While fashioning his lines he'd scratch   70
his head repeatedly and chew his nails away to nothing.
Keep reversing your pencil if you'd like to write a piece
worth reading twice, and don't work to please the crowd.
Enjoy a small circle of readers. Or are you mad,
and want your poems recited in every little school?   75
I don't. I'm happy if the knights[5] applaud me, as brave
Arbuscula once said when hissed: she scorned the rest.
Why should I let that louse Pantilius get on my nerves,
or Demetrius, needling me when I'm not there, or stupid
Fannius, who tries to injure me at Tigellius's dinner?   80
Plotius and Varius, Maecenas and Vergil, Valgius,
Fuscus, and noble Octavius are those whose respect
I want to keep, along with the Viscus brothers' praise.

---

3. The iambic trimeter or scenarius, considered to have three feet, was the meter of drama, like Pollio's tragedy. See *Ars Poetica* 251–54.
4. Lucilius.

5. A social class ranked between the senators and the common people. By Horace's time it was composed largely of wealthy landowners and merchants.

Without trying to flatter anyone, I can mention you,
Pollio, and you and your brother, Messalla. I can name you,   85
Bibulus and Servius, and, truthful Furnius, you too.
There are many other literate men who are my friends,
but I can't name every one. It's their esteem I seek
for all I write, and if they're less happy than I hoped,
I regret it. So, Demetrius, and Tigellius, you too,   90
scream on in good health around your lady pupils' chairs.
Go, Boy, be quick. Enter these lines in my little book.

Book II

1

Horace: To some my satire seems too cutting, so extreme
it violates the law; others think that nothing I write
has any strength to it, and that a thousand lines like mine
could be spun out in a day. Trebatius, what do you suggest?
Trebatius: That you clam up. *Hor:* You mean, never write anything   5
at all? *Treb:* Exactly. *Hor:* It kills me to reject a tip
as good as that, but, you see, I can't sleep. *Treb:* Thrice, oiled,
transnavigate the Tiber if you require sound sleep;
and then be sure your body's soaked in wine by night.
Or if such great love of writing grips you, think big;   10
sing about unbeaten Caesar's deeds, and be rewarded.
Hor: Exactly what I'd like, best of fathers, but in strength
I'm insufficient; we all can't write of battle lines
prickly with lances or dying Gauls with broken spears,
or show a wounded Parthian falling from his horse.   15
Treb: Then write about his justice and his ability to rule;
wise Lucilius did that for Scipio. *Hor:* There I won't fail myself,
when the moment comes. But until then Flaccus's[1] words
in Caesar's ear won't seek reception, for if you touch him
without care, he'll guard himself by kicking on all sides.   20
Treb: That's much better than wounding with your surly lines
Pantolabus the leech and Nomentanus the spendthrift,[2]
for all fear you, even those untouched, and hate you.
Hor: What can I do? Milonius dances when he's drunk, the heat
increasing in his boiled brains, the lamps before his eyes.   25
Castor's joy is horses, his identical egg-mate[3] loves boxing;
of the thousand things that men like doing, each man
finds his own. My pleasure is arranging words in meter
in the style of Lucilius, a better man than you or I.
Long ago he made his books his faithful friends and to them   30
trusted his most private thoughts. In good fortune and bad,
he never rushed to other confidants. So, in his work we see,
as if upon a votive tablet,[4] the old man's entire life.
Him I follow, unsure if I'm Lucanian or Apulian,
for Venusia's farmers plow along both borders, sent in   35
after the Samnites were expelled—that's the tradition—
to keep Rome's enemies from filling up the empty space,
two fierce peoples, Apulians and Lucanians, threatening war.
But my pen will never jab without a provocation
at anyone on earth, for it protects me like a sword   40
kept in the sheath. Why should I ever pull it out

---

1. The names of Roman citizens were characteristically
tripartite, composed of the *praenomen* or personal
name, the *nomen* or clan-name, and an additional name
called the *cognomen*. Horace's cognomen was Flaccus.
2. An echo of Horace's own *S*.I.8.11.
3. The twins Castor and Pollux (see Glossary) were

born from the union of Leda and Zeus, who had taken
the form of a swan.
4. An escape from some threatening situation, such as
illness or shipwreck, was often commemorated by a
tablet, affixed to a temple wall, which told the story by
means of a picture.

if no criminal attacks me? Jupiter, Father and King,
may my weapon stay unused and perish from rust,
and no one injure me. I'm a lover of peace. But any guy
who gives me any trouble (my motto is "Hands off!")   45
will become a tearful celebrity, sung about all over town.
When Cervius is angry he'll get you through the courts.
Canidia keeps Albucius's poison for those she hates.
Expect a heavy fine from Turius, if he's your judge.
Each of us has a special way of fighting enemies,   50
and sovereign nature orders all. Let me explain.
Wolves fight with teeth, bulls with horns. What taught them,
if not instinct? Give to spendthrift Scaeva his old mother
to take care of, and his pious hand will strike no blow. Odd?
No odder than that wolves don't kick and bulls don't bite.   55
He'll use honey on the old lady, with a dash of hemlock.
Here's my point. Whether peaceful aging lies ahead
or death now hovers over me, circling on black wings,
wealthy or poor, in Rome or, as fate wills it, in exile,
whatever my life's color, I'll write. *Treb:* Son, I'm concerned   60
about your life's length: someone highly placed may strike you
with a deadly chill. *Hor:* What! When Lucilius, first
to compose poems of this kind, dared to strip the skins
from those who dazzled all the men they walked among,
though filthy underneath, did Laelius or the great man   65
who well deserved the name he took from conquered Carthage[5]
dislike his wit? Were they sorry Metellus was hurt,
Lupus pelted, by poems that exposed them? And *he* arraigned
the people's leaders and all the people, tribe by tribe,
since he favored virtue only and virtue's friends.   70
Why, when they vacationed from the crowded public scene,
valiant Scipio and wise and kindly Laelius always liked
to have him there too, in their retreats. They joked together
while the cabbage cooked. Whatever I am, no matter how
inferior to Lucilius in talent and in rank, I too   75
have lived among the great, as envy must admit;
seeking a soft morsel to sink her teeth into, she'll bite
on something hard in me—unless you, Trebatius,
think I'm wrong. *Treb:* No, I can't find holes in your defense.
But still, I warn you to be careful: you can cause yourself   80
big trouble by not knowing about our sacred laws;
if one party composes bad poems about another, we have
a procedure and a penalty. *Hor:* Yes, if they're bad,
but what if they're good and praised by Caesar? What if,
though I've barked at those worth barking at, I'm guiltless?   85
Treb: The court will dismiss the charges with a laugh, and you too.

2

What and how much, my friends, simple living offers
(I'm not doing the talking; this is a lesson from Ofellus,[1]

---

5. Scipio Aemilianus Africanus, who achieved the final defeat of Carthage, the great Phoenician colony on the coast of North Africa.

1. An old peasant whose ideas on life and food Horace relates until line 116, when he allows Ofellus to speak for himself.

a farmer unschooled but wise, with lots of common sense),
learn here, with no gleaming plates and silverware around.
All that shiny stuff will dazzle and disorder you, tilt   5
your soul towards falsehood, make it reject what is better.
Here we search for truth, without our lunch. "Why do that?"
I'll do my best to tell you. Truth is never fairly weighed
by a bribed judge. Hunt rabbits, ride a spirited horse:
get tired. Or if Roman martial sports are just too rough   10
for someone used to Greece's games, play catch; throw hard,
it's fun, and you'll never notice how much work it is.
If you like the discus, slice the unresisting air with that.
Then, hungry and dry, the snot beaten out of you by work,
try scorning plain food or mead not made of Hymettian honey,   15
Falernian wine. Your chef's gone out and the ocean, black
and in a fury, guards its fish. Bread and salt are good enough
to ease your growling gut. Why do you think this happens,
what causes it? Eating's highest pleasure lies in you,
not in the flavor of your food. Make it taste good   20
by sweating first. A pulpy, pale gourmet won't like
his oysters or fine fish or grouse from overseas.
Well, I'll hardly persuade you, if peacock is served,
not to tickle your tongue with that instead of chicken.
You're bribed by false considerations, by its price   25
as a rare bird, by the showy, painted tail it spreads,
as if these things mattered. Do you eat the feathers
that you praise? Cooked, is the bird a decoration still?
Peacock and chicken taste the same, but you fool yourself
and pick the prettier bird. That I can understand,   30
but what instinct tells you if a gaping pike is Tiber caught
or deep sea, whether it swam around between the bridges
inside Rome or at the river's mouth? Madman, you praise
a three-pound mullet, which must be sliced before you eat.
I get it. You're attracted by the size. Why then do you   35
detest long pikes? Here's the reason: only because
nature made one fish large and made the other small.
Rarely does an unstuffed stomach despise normal foods.
"A big fish laid out on a big platter—that's a sight
I appreciate," says Cramgut, honorary harpy. Come on,   40
strong southern winds, cook his dinner your way! But no,
boar and turbot rot fresh inside his belly, whose fullness
makes it sick; it's so tight crammed it cries for radishes
and sour pickles. Not every food that poor men eat
have our royal tables banned, not yet. Plain eggs,   45
black olives, still have a role today. When, not long ago,
Gallonius the auctioneer served sturgeon, he gave his table
a bad name. "Oh? Did the seas hold fewer turbot then?"[2]
Safe was the turbot and safe was the stork in its nest
until our leader the praetor taught you different. I'm sure   50

2. The current fad of serving turbot has become so natural to this interlocutor that he cannot imagine a time
when tastes were different or more sensible.

if someone now decreed the tastiness of roasted gull,
Rome's youth, docile students of debauchery, would obey.
A stingy life is most unlike a simple one, Ofellus thinks,
since you don't profit at all by escaping one vice
if you're then perverted by its opposite. Avidienus,   55
who has been labeled "Dog," a nickname truly earned,
eats olives aged five years and cornel berries,
is very sparing with his wine until it's turned, and his oil
has a stink you couldn't bear. He will allow himself
at wedding feasts, birthday parties, and other occasions   60
of joy, to celebrate in formal white, oiling the salad
from his kitchen horn, in drops, and pouring on old vinegar.
Which way of life should the wise man follow? Which example
imitate? That's choosing between a wolf's life and a dog's.
A wise man will be sensible, not disgustingly cheap,   65
and not ruin his life by either extreme. He won't be savage
to his slaves, as old Albucius was, before dinner even started,
or imitate dim-witted Naevius who supplied his guests
with greasy water. That is a very serious offense.
I'll tell you now what and how much simple living gives.   70
First it brings good health; for eating different things
can hurt a man, don't you agree? You remember how easily
your stomach once held simple foods. But when you mix
roasted meats with boiled and shellfish with thrushes,
sweet turns to sour and within your belly rolls a storm,   75
borne on thick and phlegmy waves. See how sickly pale
the diners rise from their hesitation feast[3]? Each body
will still be loaded down tomorrow from tonight's excess,
the souls too, bits of divine spirit fastened to the ground.
But someone wise, who treats his body right, falls asleep   80
before you can say boo and he gets up ready to work.
This man can always break his pattern and celebrate
when a holiday comes up, brought by the circling year.
Or, if he wants, he can pamper himself when sick
and relieve the feeble end of life with easy treatment.   85
But since you got started too early, when your health
was perfectly all right, how much softer can you have it
when bad health moves in on you, or wearying old age?
Our fathers praised a rancid boar, not because their faces
lacked a nose, but, I believe, for this reason: so guests   90
arriving late could eat the spoiled meat. That was better
than the gluttonous host gobbling it all up fresh. I wish
I'd been born when the earth was new, among those men.
Do you care about having a good name, which sounds better
in men's ears than any song? Huge dinners and huge turbot   95
bring huge disgrace, coupled with financial loss. Throw in
your angry uncle, the neighbors, your self-hatred,
your death-craving (in vain, since you won't have a cent

---

3. A dinner so sumptuous and varied that the guests
cannot decide what to eat first. The phrase was used by
the comic poet Terence (*Phormio* 342), and by Horace's
time had become proverbial.

to buy a rope). "All right," you say, "scold Trausius
like this, not me. My income's immense and I'm as rich   100
as any three kings." If that's so, and you have more
money than you need, why not spend it in a better way?
Why is anyone poor who shouldn't be, if you're so rich?
Why do the gods' old temples need repair? You ingrate,
for your beloved country's sake can't you dip into your stash?   105
I know, you always come out on top, the great exception.
Well, someday your enemies will laugh and laugh. Consider:
life is full of changes, and who can stand them better? A man
who treats his body and proud mind to luxury, addicting them,
or someone used to little and to thinking of the future,   110
a man wise in peacetime, preparing then the tools of war?
You can believe all this, because when I knew Ofellus
in my youth he lived, on his own land, no better than now,
as a tenant. See him on the little farm they took away,
his animals and sons there with him, a tough old hired hand.   115
"I never used to eat," he says, "on an average working day
anything but some cabbage and the end of a smoked ham.
But if after long absence a friend would come to visit
or a welcome neighbor, on rainy days when we couldn't work,
we used to eat well, not on fish shipped from the city   120
but on chicken and kid. The dessert tables had raisins
and nuts to dress them up, and some split figs too.
Last came a drinking game with each man his own master[4]
and a toast for Ceres—'Rise high on towering stalk'—
as she unknit with wine the wrinkles on our brows.   125
Rage though fortune may and start new confusion working,
how can she diminish that? How have I suffered, or you,
my sons, in health and spirit, since the new man came?
The land has no owners: nature never granted him a title,
she gave no rights to me or anyone. He pushed us out;   130
his sloth, or his ignorance of our complicated law,
a surviving heir, if nothing else, will push him out.
Now this field is named after Umbrenus; Ofellus was
the old name. It belongs to no one, but lets itself be used
now by me, now by others. So then, live, live and endure.   135
Meet life's difficulties with strong, enduring hearts."

31

Damasippus: Your production stinks. All of four times a year
you call for paper, and then you just revise old work,
angry at yourself because, far too fond of wine and sleep,
you write nothing people talk about. What will become of you?
At Saturnalia[2] time you flee out here. You're sober, begin!   5

4. Instead of observing banquet protocol by selecting a drinking-master to prescribe rules for their drinking, they were guided only by their individual sense of propriety. Cf. *S.II.6.67–70.*

1. A dialogue between Horace and Junius Damasippus, an antique dealer and real estate agent who is also mentioned in Cicero's *Letters.* Damasippus rebukes Horace for his laziness, and relates how he himself was prevented from committing suicide and was immediately converted to Stoicism by the intervention of Stertinius. Damasippus relates the sage's lengthy rescue-sermon, based on the Stoic precept "everyone except the sage is mad," in 38–295; and in 307–325 he explains why Horace specifically is mad.

2. A festival beginning on December 17, characterized by feasting, exchange of gifts, and special liberties for slaves. Horace is spending the Saturnalia on his Sabine farm.

You're here to write, so write. See, you don't even try.
Blaming your pen won't help and it's wrong to hit the wall,
which, since its creation, has angered gods and poets.
You had a look that said, "I promise many shining poems;
just let me be, covered by my little farm's warm roof."   10
What was the point of taking with you Plato and Menander,
Eupolis and Archilochus, of bringing such important friends?
You think you can appease ill will by not preaching virtue?
Idiot, that's the way to be despised! Flee that evil siren
Sloth, or what your good conduct has gained you, prepare   15
with balanced mind to lose. *Horace:* Damasippus, may the gods
and goddesses send you, for such good advice, a barber.[3]
But what makes you a Horace expert? *Dam:* Since my total wreck
at Janus's middle arch[4] I've dealt in others' business,
knocked overboard from mine. I enjoyed it so much once,   20
guessing that a copper pot was a foot-bath for sly Sisyphus,
or deciding which piece was rudely carved, which roughly cast.
They were worth fortunes if I, the expert, said so.
And elegant homes and gardens—only I understood the way
to buy them and save money. I was "Mercury's Boy."   25
That's what people called me on the streets. *Hor:* I remember,
and I'm amazed to see you cured of that disease. *Dam:* Yes,
it's amazing how the new dislodged the old, like a pain
moving from your head or side into your belly
or a catatonic patient suddenly slugging his physician.   30
Hor: Do whatever you want, just don't do that. *Dam:* My friend, don't
get the wrong idea; you're mad, as nearly all fools are,
if Stertinius jabbered true in those amazing words,
that wisdom which I dutifully wrote down the very day
he gave me comfort, instructing me to grow a wise man's beard,   35
to leave the Fabrician Bridge and be no longer sad.
After going broke, I thought I'd cover up my head and jump
into the river, but he appeared to save me. "Beware," he said,
"don't sell yourself short. Your agonizing shame is false;
you're afraid that men will think you mad, buty *they're* mad.   40
First, let's see what madness is; if it exists in you alone,
I won't delay a brave man's death with further words.
Anyone whom gross stupidity and ignorance of truth
make blind will be judged insane by Chrysippus's school
and flock. This is so for both common men and great,   45
for all men but philosophers. Now, hear why you're no madder
than all those others, who bestowed on you the name
'insane.' Think of travelers in a forest who get lost
and leave the proper path: one might wander over
to the left, the other to the right. They're deceived   50
in different ways, but it's the same mistake. Similarly,
you think you're insane, but who is any wiser
among those tail-draggers[5] who make fun of you? One kind

---

3. Damasippus, like other philosophers, has grown a long, flowing beard.
4. Used of the banking and commerce district of the Forum, located near one of the arches named after Janus, the god of entrances, beginnings, and new undertakings.
5. Children often played a trick on someone by tying a tail to his backside without his knowing it. Cf. 299.

of fool is frightened when there's nothing to fear. He bawls
that fires, rocks, and rivers block his way, on an open plain.   55
A different type, though just as nutty, dashes into fires
or straight into rivers while his loving mother screams,
together with his worthy sister, his cousins, father, and his wife:
'That's a huge ditch, a gigantic cliff! Hey, watch out!'
But he'll listen no more than drunken Fufius[6] once did,   60
that snoring Iliona, deaf while twelve hundred Catieni
roared, 'Mother, I'm calling you.' All ordinary people,
as I'll show you, are just as crazy as those two.
He's gone mad, Damasippus has, with buying old statues,
but is the mind of his creditor intact? I wonder.   65
'Here, take what you'll never give back.' If *I* say that,
are *you* crazy for taking the money? Are you crazier
than if you didn't take what Mercury so kindly brought?
Write ten notes to Nerius—not enough. Have Cicuta add
a hundred more to tie up loose ends, add a thousand chains.   70
No matter how he's held, shifty Proteus gets away.
When you take him into court he'll only laugh at you,
and become anything he likes, boar, bird, rock, or tree.
If a clever deal is sane and a stupid one insane,
the mind that's really gone is Perellius's, believe me,   75
for he lent you money you couldn't possibly repay.
'Settle yourself and listen well.' So I order everyone
turned sickly pale by warped ambition or by lust for cash,
all who run a fever from high living, or superstition,
or any other illness that may affect the mind. Come closer,   80
and I'll explain why you're all mad. Come on, get in line.
Give the biggest dose of hellebore,[7] by all means, to misers;
I doubt reason would err in giving them all Anticyra.
Staberius's sons carved the total of his fortune on his tomb:
it was either that or, as a forfeit, give the people   85
two hundred gladiators in a show, a monstrous feast,
and an Egyptian quantity of grain. 'Whether I made
a sane or crazy will, don't *you* presume to judge.' It seems
that wise Staberius doubted their enthusiasm. But what
did he intend by making them inscribe their patrimony   90
on his stone? All through his life he considered poverty
a hideous crime; nothing frightened him more, and had he
died with his fortune a penny smaller than it was,
he'd have thought himself a lesser man. 'But don't all things,
virtue, a good name, honor, all that's human and divine,   95
obey money, lovely money? Whoever has a pile of it
is famous, strong and just.' And wise? 'Right, and a king,
whatever he wants.' That miser expected from posterity

---

6. In Pacuvius' tragedy *Iliona*, the spirit of Iliona's
murdered son came to her as she was sleeping to reproach her and ask for proper burial. In one performance the actor Fufius, who as Iliona was supposed to
awake and reply, was so drunk that the spirit of her son,
played by Catienus, was not able to wake her. The

audience then joined in, chanting Catienus' line,
"Mother, I'm calling you."

7. A plant produced around the town of Anticyra (83)
in Phocis, supposed to cure madness through its violent
effects on the digestive system.

great praise, as if he'd hoarded virtue, not money. How did
he differ from Aristippus, the Greek? His servants littered
the desert with his gold, at his request. They were too slow
beneath its weight. Who was madder, he or Staberius?
It's pointless to cure one problem by creating another.
If someone started buying and collecting harps,
but didn't like them or even like music, or bought
awls and lasts, though not a shoemaker, or ship's canvas
when he didn't intend to make a trip, all would call him
foolish and insane, what else? But how would he differ
from a man who gathered stores of gold and silver, ignorant
of money's use, fearing to touch it as if it were divine?
Suppose the owner of a gigantic heap of corn stayed up
on constant guard, armed with a heavy stick, and never dared,
though it was his and he was hungry, to touch one grain,
choosing to live on bitter leaves instead and nearly starve?
Suppose, with Chian and old Falernian in the cellar,
a thousand casks—no, three hundred thousand—he drank
sharp vinegar? Yes, and lay on straw, pushing eighty
we'll say he is, while his bedclothes stayed locked
and rotting in a chest, providing food to moths and bugs.
You know, few men would think him mad, and this is why:
nearly all of mankind suffers from the same disease.
Are you saving it for a son to waste, or perhaps, old man
hated by the gods, only a slave? Or just to stay covered?
How much money would you lose if you began each day
by smearing your greens with better oil, also your head,
that dirty, snarled mass of flakes? And why is it,
when no one needs more than enough, you lie, thieve, and rob
each chance you get. You're sane? If you started pitching stones
at people, or at your own slaves that cost good money,
every little boy and girl would shriek that you were mad.
But when you choke your wife or give your mother poison,
are you being sane? You are? Oh, you're not in Argos
and don't kill mother with a sword, unlike mad Orestes.[8]
Then you must believe he went insane after he killed her,
and that the foul Furies didn't madden him until he's warmed
within his mother's throat the sharp point of his sword.
The truth is that after people thought Orestes was mad,
he really did nothing for which you could reproach him.
He didn't dare slash Pylades with his sword, or his sister
Electra, but only showered curses on them both, calling her
a fury and him something else, suggested by his bile.
Poor Mr. Rich, with lots of silver and gold, well-hidden,
had a custom of drinking Veientine red on holidays,
but usually, out of his clay dipper, he drank dregs.

100

105

110

115

120

125

130

135

140

---

8. The Stoic takes exception to the common supposi-
tion that madness reveals itself through violence or
through conspicuously erratic behavior. Thus the man
who quietly does away with his mother by poison is as
mad as the legendary Orestes, who killed his mother
with a sword to avenge her murder of his father. Afterwards, when driven frantic by the Furies, he was actually less insane in his actions toward his sister Electra
and his friend Pylades than when he had planned and
carried out his crime.

Once he lay crushed by a lethargy so deep his heir   145
began to dance around the chest and keys, shouting
out his joy; but the doctor, loyal and quick-thinking,
devised this cure. He had a table brought into the room
and bags of money dumped out on it; then he summoned clerks
to add it up. This revived Rich. The doctor warned him: 150
'Guard your cash; your greedy heir is taking all.'
'While I'm alive?' 'Want to live? Then listen.' 'I will.'
'Your heart will fail, weakened as you are, unless you eat
and speed to your collapsing gut great quantities of strength.
Now's the time to start. Here, have some of this rice broth.' 155
'How much?' 'It's cheap.' 'Come on, how much?' 'Eight cents.' 'Eight cents!
I have to die; if not from sickness, maybe from assault.'
'Well, who is sane?' Whoever is no fool. 'And what are misers?'
Fools and insane. 'Suppose a man isn't a miser: that means
he's sane?' Not at all. 'But Stoic, why?' I'll tell you.   160
Our patient (suppose Dr. Craterus to say) shows no signs
of stomach illness. 'Then he's well enough to rise?' No.
He could be in trouble from bad kidneys or bad lungs.
This man doesn't lie, and he's not cheap. The gods are kind,
he should offer them a pig. Oh, he's ambitious, a daredevil? 165
Send him to Anticyra for the cure. What's the difference
whether you throw your fortune away or never use it?
They say that Servius Oppidius, a very wealthy man
by former standards, divided two Canusian estates
between his sons. On his deathbed he called them in and said: 170
'When I saw you, Aulus, carrying nuts and marbles
folded in your robe, to gamble with or just to give away,
and you, Tiberius, grimly counting and hiding yours in holes,
I began to fear the effects of a divergent madness,
for you might have become a Nomentanus, you a Cicuta.   175
So, calling upon our household gods, I warn you both:
Don't you diminish, and don't you decrease your wealth
beyond nature's limits and what your father thinks enough.
And to keep away the glory itch, I'll restrain you
with a clause: if either son becomes an aedile,   180
or a praetor, he forfeits all property and rights.
Are popcorn and peanuts[9] to get votes worth such a loss
so that you can strut about the circus and have a statue made?
Stripped of your father's land, madman, and his wealth,
will you endeavor to be praised as Agrippa is praised?   185
What a clever fox you'd be to imitate a trueborn lion.'
'You forbid us all, son of Atreus,[1] to bury Ajax. But why?'
'I'm king.' 'I'm a commoner, but I'm only asking.' 'It's just,

9. Literally, chickpeas, beans, and lupine seeds, bribes to get the common people's votes.
1. Agamemnon. After the Trojan War, Ajax was bested by Odysseus (or Ulysses) in his claim for the arms of dead Achilles. In his bitterness he resolved to murder Agamemnon, Menelaus, and Odysseus, but was driven mad by Athene and slew a flock of sheep instead. When his senses were restored, he committed suicide out of shame. A dispute then ensued, in which Agamemnon and Menelaus argued that Ajax did not deserve burial, while Teucer (Ajax's brother) and Odysseus argued on Ajax's behalf. Here Stertinius takes Ajax's side, following Stoic principle by arguing that Ajax was no madder than Agamemnon himself when Agamemnon sacrificed his daughter Iphigeneia to appease the goddess Artemis and ensure fair sailing to Troy.

what I order. If anyone thinks it isn't, don't be afraid:
say what you think. I give permission.' 'Greatest of kings   190
(may the gods bring you quickly home once Troy is taken),
may I ask a question and speak my mind a little later?'
'Ask.' 'Since Ajax was, after Achilles, our greatest hero,
and often gloriously saved the Greeks, why does he lie and rot?
Is it to please Priam and his people that you won't bury him,   195
who denied graves in native ground to so many of Troy's sons?'
'That madman put a thousand sheep to death, crying out
that great Ulysses and Menelaus and I were those he killed.'
'At Aulis, when you made your daughter stand in for a calf
upon the altar, you pervert, sprinkling her with salted meal,[2]   200
was your mind then working right?' 'Well, explain.' 'How much harm
did crazy Ajax do in butchering that flock? He did no harm
to wife and son. Though he roundly cursed the Atridae,
he didn't actually hurt Teucer or even Ulysses.'
'But since my ships were stuck upon a hostile shore,   205
I got them off, wisely placating the gods with blood.'
'Your own blood, you maniac!' 'Mine, but I'm no maniac.'
Anyone who has false fantasies which are all mixed up
with criminal confusion must be considered mad.
Stupidity can make you that way as well as anger.   210
Ajax was raving when he killed those innocent lambs;
when you commit a 'wise' crime to win an empty honor,
is your mind in order, and your swelled heart free of sin?
If it pleased someone to take a chubby lamb for little rides,
address her as his daughter, give her jewelry and maids,   215
if he called her Rufa or Pusilla and wanted to land her
a nice husband, he would be ruled mentally incompetent
by the praetor and become his sane relations' ward.
Well, if someone kills his daughter instead of a dumb lamb,
is his mind working as it should? Of course not. So then,   220
an evil stupidity is madness at its peak. A wicked man
is also crazed; anyone seized by falsely gleaming fame
heard the wild thunder of bloody Bellona until he went mad.
Now then, together let's attack Nomentanus and high living,
for reason shows that spendthrifts are both foolish and insane.   225
One man, on claiming his inheritance, a thousand talents,
decreed that the sellers of fish and fruit and game,
the perfume man, the mob of crooks from Tuscus Street,
the parasites, the sausage makers, and all the market people
must see him in the morning. So all those characters came.   230
The pimp said, 'Anything I got, or that any of us got
in stock consider yours. You can take it now or later.'
Here's the answer he received from this excellent young man:
'In Lucania's snows you sleep in leggings, hunting the boar
I'll have for dinner. From the winter sea you net me fishes.   235
I'm so lazy, I don't deserve to have all this. So, here!
You, take a million, you too. And you, take triple,

2. Part of the ceremony of sacrificing an animal.

since your wife comes running at midnight when I call.'
The son of Aesopus wanted to swallow a cool million,
so he plucked a pearl from Metella's ear, then in vinegar   240
dissolved the precious stone. Was he saner than if he'd
tossed the pearl into a rushing stream, or sewer?
Quintus Arrius had two sons, a fine fraternal pair,
in spending and fooling, in love of the perverse, true twins.
They ate nightingales for breakfast, bought at vast expense.   245
Should we consider them happily sane or miserably mad?
Building houses of cards, hitching mice to a toy wagon,
playing odds and evens, going for rides on rocking horses—
a grown man would be crazy if he enjoyed these things.
If reason could show you that love is more childish yet,   250
and that it's no sillier to play kid games in the dust
than to complain about your love life with some whore,
I wonder if you would act the way converted Polemon
once did and shed the signs of your disease, your modish garters,
elbow pads, and scarves? The story is that he,   255
though drunk, quickly pulled the garlands from his neck
the moment his sober teacher's words made him a different man.
Offer a snotty kid an apple, he'll reject you. 'Here, kid.'
'Naw!' If you didn't offer it, he'd want it. A lover scorned
is little different, wondering if he should or shouldn't go   260
where he's not been asked and would have to sit outside
those hated doors. 'But now, now that she's asked me, should I go?
Or would it be wiser just to end this pain I suffer?
She rejects me, recalls me. Go back? No, not if she begs!'
Here's his slave, much wiser. 'Young sir, these affairs   265
don't make sense and can't be planned; all reason and order
they deny. That's the way love goes, now it's war,
then peace. It's very changeable, like stormy weather,
and it operates in fits and starts, by blind chance.
To make love fit some fixed ideas would work as well   270
as going crazy by a plan, according to set rules.'
Why? If, when flipping apple seeds,[3] you get a charge
when one raps on the ceiling, is that self-control?
Why do you think? You lisp of love through toothless gums:
are you saner than an architect of cards? Add blood   275
to madness, and you stir fire with a sword. Not long ago
Marius stabbed his sweetheart, then plunged to his own death.
Was Marius mad? Or do you acquit him of this charge,
that he had a disturbed mind, and judge he's only bad,
as people do, giving the same condition different names?   280
A freed slave used to run to all the temples every morning
(not a drunk, just an old man with washed hands): 'One man—
that's not very much at all—one man, me, save from dying.
For gods that's easy!' So he prayed. Though unimpaired
in eye and ear, unless his first owner liked being sued,   285

3. To hit the ceiling with an apple seed shot from between thumb and forefinger was considered an omen of luck in love.

his madness was mentioned at his sale. Superstitious folks
are also part, Chrysippus says, of mad Menenius's fruitful tribe.
'O Jupiter, who gives and takes away all sorrows,'
a mother says, her son lying sick five months;
'If these malarial chills will leave my boy, the morning   290
of the fasting day which you've decreed, I'll dip him, stripped,
into the Tiber.' If luck or the doctor gets the patient
through the worst, the crazy mother will execute her son,
placing him on the icy bank and bringing back the fever.
What evil thing impaired her mind? She feared the gods."   295
So spoke Stertinius, the eighth sage, to me, his friend,
arming me so that name callers won't henceforth escape.
Whoever dares call me insane will hear as much from me,
and learn to see what he didn't know was dangling from his butt.
Horace: Stoic—oh, good luck on selling your remaining goods,   300
at a profit—which folly, since there's more than one,
do you think proves me insane? For I strike myself as sane.
Damasippus: What? When Agave carries in her hands the head she ripped
from her poor son, do you think she knows she's mad?
Hor: I'm a fool. I confess it, since truth should be respected,   305
and also insane. But could you please explain which vice,
in your opinion, reveals my mind's disease? *Dam:* Listen, first
you're building, so you're copying the big boys, though from top
to bottom you stand all of two feet tall. Still, despite that,
little Turbo makes you laugh because his spirit, his fire   310
in battle, is larger than his body. Are you any less absurd?
Whatever Maecenas does, is it appropriate that you,
so unlike him and so much smaller, should be his rival?
When their mother was away a calf trampled some young frogs.
One escaped and was telling the mother how a huge beast,   315
a monster, had wiped out the whole family, when she asked:
"How big was it?" and puffed herself up. "This big?"
"Twice as big." "This big?" she asked, as she inflated
more and more. "You couldn't match it," he said, "if you popped."
That doesn't fit you at all badly, that little scene.   320
Now, toss in the poems, that is, toss oil on flames.
If anyone sane ever wrote such things, you just might be too.
I won't mention your rotten temper—*Hor:* Hey, enough! *Dam:* And
your overspending. *Hor:* Stick you to your own affairs, Damasippus.
Dam: Your mad lusts for a thousand girls, a thousand boys.   325
Hor: O greater one, greater madman, please spare the lesser.

4

Horace: Where've you been, Catius? And where are you going?
Catius: Sorry, I've got to write up this new philosophy;
it makes Pythagoras, Socrates, and clever Plato all look sick.
Hor: This isn't a good time to bother you, I can tell,
but since I'm a friend of yours, I hope that you'll forgive me.   5
Besides, anything that you forget, you'll soon recall
with your great memory, that miracle of nature or of art.

Cat: Well, that's the problem, how to remember everything.
It was a complex doctrine, expressed in subtle terms.
Hor: Tell me your teacher's name and if he's a foreigner or Roman.   10
Cat: I'll recite his precepts from memory, their author hide.
The long, less round eggs are preferable; so, be sure,
since they taste better and are whiter than the round,
that you serve them (and, they're hard and have male yolks).
Cabbage from near Rome doesn't equal that from drier ground.   15
Nothing has a flatter taste than greens from wet gardens.
If some night a sudden guest should catch you unprepared,
be smart; don't serve up a wiry hen resistant to his teeth,
but plunge it, before you kill it, in dilute Falernian wine.
That makes it tender. Get mushrooms grown in meadows,   20
they're the best; don't trust the others. Healthy summers
are assured a man who eats black mulberry desserts,
berries gathered from the tree before the sun gets high.
Aufidius used strong Falernian blended with his honey;
an error, since it's best to put into an empty belly   25
nothing that isn't bland. A bland mead is superior
for cleaning out the system. If your bowels get hard and lock,
mussels can drive obstructions out, any shellfish can.
(Low-growing sorrel too, if you take it with white Coan wine.)
Those slimy shellfish get fatter as the moon gets fuller,   30
but not every sea produces the best specimens.
Baiae's purple-fish beat Lake Lucrine's giant mussels,
good oysters come from Circeii, urchins from Misenum,
and sweet Tarentum brags about its broad-shelled scallops.
No one should rashly claim he knows the art of giving dinners   35
without studying the underlying science first, that of flavor,
for it won't help to net expensive fish at market
if the host doesn't know which need sauces and which,
simply broiled, will revive the faded hunger of a guest.
An Umbrian boar, acorn fed, will bend the platters   40
of gourmets, who won't serve meat that has no taste,
for Laurentian boar is bad, fattened on rushes and on reeds.
Deer who've grazed in vineyards aren't always fit to eat.
From the prolific rabbit a wise man picks the forelegs.
What the age and quality of fish and birds should be,   45
no sense of taste before mine ever really understood;
some men have just enough talent to invent a new cookie.
But it's never right to make one thing your only care;
you can worry so much about your wine, for instance,
that you don't use the right oil for basting the fish.   50
If you put Massic wines outside on a clear night, they lose
any roughness they may have, for the evening air refines them
and kills the odor, strong enough to do damage to one's nerves.
But note: filtered through linen, their flavor won't be pure.
A smart gourmet pours Falernian lees into Surrentine wine,   55
then drops a dove's egg in to get what won't dissolve;
as the yolk sinks down, it tidily gathers every bit.

Fried prawns will revive a guest's interest in your wine,
African snails will too. After drinking, lettuce just sits
inside a queasy stomach, which needs a spur, sausage or ham,   60
to get it back in shape again. You can get the same effect
with something hot and greasy from a neighborhood café.
Culinary triumph will reward your careful study of the sauce
whose nature is twofold. A simple base: sweet olive oil
into which you blend, to make it right, thick wine and brine   65
but only that which stunk before in a jar of pickled fish.
Stir the mixture well and set to boiling with chopped herbs;
then sprinkle with Corycian saffron, and finish up
by adding oil pressed from highest grade Venafran olives.
Picenian fruit has less flavor than fruit from Tibur,   70
though it looks better. You should store Venuculan grapes
in pots, but smoke Albans and dry them into raisins.
I first served these with apples. I first mixed caviar and lees,[1]
and I was also first to pass white pepper and black salt
around the table, each sifted on a private plate.   75
It's criminal to pay three thousand sesterces for fish
that roved the seas, then cram them on a narrow plate.
It really makes you sick to see a slave with greasy paws,
from licking at some food he thieved, pick up a cup,
or to find a coating of old filth inside an antique bowl.   80
Plain brooms, place mats, sawdust—just how expensive
are these simple things? Not to have them is a great disgrace.
Do you scrape mosaic floors with a muddy palm whisk
and throw dirty wraps on couches covered with fine cloth?
You forget that since neatness is both cheap and easy,   85
you're more justly blamed for lacking that one quality
than any fancy item found only on the tables of the rich.
Hor: Professor Catius, I beg you as my friend, please the gods
and me: take me to a lecture, no matter where. Don't forget!
You could bring me your retentive memory's total store,   90
but as a middleman you won't wholly satisfy me. Besides,
it matters how he looks and acts. To you, you lucky dog,
that's not so important, but you've seen him. Not slight
is my desire to approach this spring, now so remote,
and drink the precepts in that make a happy life.   95

5[1]

Ulysses: This too, Tiresias, besides telling me I'll return,
answer me this: how can I recoup my losses, what tricks
and tactics can I use? You laugh? *Tiresias:* What an operator!
It's not enough to sail back home to Ithaka and see
your father's gods once more? *Ul:* O, liar to no man,   5
you know I'll get there broke and naked: you foretold it.
The suitors haven't left my herd or cellar whole; and

---

1. The tartar crust or sediment which wine deposits
during fermentation and aging, used in Horace's time as
a pungent condiment.

1. This satire is a modernized version of Tiresias'
counseling of Odysseus (Ulysses is the Latin version of
the name) in *Odyssey* XI. Here Odysseus wants to
recover his lost fortune, and Tiresias advises him on the
widespread Roman practice of legacy hunting.

birth and valor, without wealth, are less than seaweed.
Tir: I won't mince words; since poverty makes you shudder so,
I'll tell you how to get ahead. If you receive a thrush   10
or something else that's nice, it's best to let it fly away
to an old man whose fortune glitters. Let him taste
your apples and other garden fruit before you give some
to your god.[2] He's holier than your god, he's rich.
It doesn't matter if he lied in court, sprang from nothing,   15
murdered his own brother or ran away from servitude,
don't refuse him, if he asks, your presence on his outer side.
Ul: I should cover dirty Dama's[3] side? *That* I never did
at Troy; only the best men were good enough for me. *Tir:* Then
you'll be broke. *Ul:* My sturdy heart I'll order to endure,   20
at times I've borne worse.[4] Go on—tell me all I need
to rake the profits in, in piles! Talk, prophet!
Tir: Talk? I've been talking. Listen: hunt old folks' wills.
Be cunning and be thorough. And if someone's wise enough
to cheat your lurking hook by escaping with the bait,   25
don't abandon hope or quit the game. What's one defeat?
In a legal battle, large or small, raging in the Forum,
one contestant may be rich, childless, and shameless,
bold enough to sue a better man. That's the fellow
you defend, not the citizen with the better name and case   30
who has a son at home or a fertile wife to give him one.
Say "Quintus" or "Publius" (for first names bring delight
to tender ears), "Your great merit has won me for your friend.
I understand our maze of laws, and I'll take on your case.
They could tear my eyes out before I'd let you look stupid   35
or lose so much as one red cent. I guarantee it:
You won't lose, and you won't be laughed at." Send him home
to file his nails while you take over, handle everything.
Hang on rock steady whether "the flaming dog star makes
the speechless statues crack," or, stuffed full of fatty tripe,   40
Furius "sputters out white snow upon the Alps in winter."[5]
"Look," someone standing there will say, elbowing another,
"there's real persistence for you, and friendship, and brains."
Then more fish will swim along and your preserves will grow.
Here's another point: if a man has a sickly son and heir,   45
one destined for abundant wealth, don't always be obvious,
courting bachelors so that you're nakedly exposed. Go slowly,
creep along and be obliging until named the second heir,
and then, if some mishap occurs to send the boy to Orcus,
you can fill the gap. Very rarely will this gamble fail.   50
If anyone offers to let you read his will, just shrug
and push the tablets back. Don't foul up on this.
But sneak a passing glance at tablet one, line two,

2. In the Latin, *lar* (see *lares* in Glossary).
3. See *S.I.6.38* and note.
4. An echo of *Odyssey* XX.18, where Odysseus coun-
sels himself to wait for the proper moment to attack the
suitors, a heroic action.

5. Horace quotes some turgid examples of contemporary epic poetry. In the second quotation, he substitutes
the poet's name, Furius, for "Jupiter" as the subject of
"sputters." See *S.I.10.36* and note.

which states if the heir is multiple or you alone.
Read that as quickly as you can. Often a police judge,   55
reboiled and made a notary, will trick a gaping crow,
and legacy poacher Nasica will make Coranus laugh.[6]
Ul: Are you crazy, or kidding me, chanting gibberish?
Tir: O Laertes' son, what I say either will be or it won't.
Great Apollo gave me my prophetic gift, remember that.   60
Ul: But explain, if that's allowable, just what it means.
Tir: When a youth to make the Parthians tremble, great Aeneas'
distant son,[7] will be supreme on both the land and sea,
then brave Coranus will take a lanky bride; for her father,
Nasica, will owe Coranus some money he'd rather not repay.   65
Then the son-in-law will offer his will to the father-in-law
and beg him to read it. Nasica will refuse many times,
but finally he'll accept, silently read, and find
his family left with nothing but good reason to complain.
My next commandment: if a scheming woman or a freed slave   70
is working on a maundering old man, make her or him a friend.
Praise them in their absence, and they'll praise you.
That helps, but the technique superior by far is to storm
the citadel direct. He's a moron and writes bad poems.
Praise them. He whores around; don't be asked, freely offer   75
Penelope to Mister Big, volunteer her. *Ul:* You think
she'll go along with that? She's so pure, so faithful,
the suitors can't dislodge her from the rightful path.
Tir: Because those cheap kids show up without big presents,
less eager for loving than for something good to eat,   80
that's why she's faithful; but if you and she just once
divide up one old man and she gets a taste of profit,
you'll never push that bitch off the greasy hide again.[8]
Listen to this: when I was old, a decadent doyenne
in Thebes left burial directions in her will: her corpse,   85
well-greased, lay on the naked shoulders of her heir.
She hoped that she might slip away in death; I guess
he must have stayed too close in life. So advance with care.
Don't stop trying, but be careful not to push too hard.
Grouchy old farts dislike a lot of talk; don't overdo it though,   90
by being silent. Imitate Davus, the slave in the comedies,
and appear respectful by standing with your head down.
Be dutiful, it pays off; warn him, if there's a breeze,
to carefully cloak his precious head. Save him from crowds,
by shouldering out a path. To his croakings cup your ear.   95
He loves praise and has to have it. Until he finally says,
"Oh, stop it!" and tosses up his hands, don't quit talking.

6. After being a mere police judge, Coranus became a notary in the civil service. The "legacy poacher Nasica" is referred to as a crow in an allusion to Aesop's fable in which the fox outwits the greedy crow. This contemporary event is related in the obscure and pompous style of an oracle.
7. A reference to Octavian (see Glossary), couched in the ambiguous langauge of prophecy. After his victory at Actium, he was expected to take vengeance on the Parthians for their defeat of the Roman general Crassus in 53 B.C. Like his adopted father, Julius Caesar, Octavian claimed descent from Aeneas, the legendary founder of the Roman race.
8. Like the bone from which, in the English expression, a dog resists separation.

Puff him up, bloated bladder of a man, with swollen words.
When he ends your lengthy term of servitude and care,
and you hear—though wide awake—"Ulysses is one heir 100
of the four," say: "Then it's true that Dama, my comrade,
is no more? Where can I find another so strong, so true?"
Throw lines like that around and, if possible, cry.
Hide your face when you have to smile. If it's your job
to bury him, don't be cheap, for a fancy funeral 105
will win the praise of everyone around. If another,
perhaps older heir develops a bad cough, mention
that if he'd like having either the fields or house
that you inherited you'll gladly take a token sum. Well,
bossy Proserpina wants me in. Live on, and good luck." 110

6

I prayed for this[1]: a measure of land, not very big,
with a garden and, by the house, a spring whose waters
never cease, and a wood just above. Greater than this
the gods have wrought, and better. Good. I ask for nothing more,
Maia's son[2]; only that you make these gifts permanently mine. 5
I haven't enlarged my property by swindling anyone
or made it smaller through waste or through neglect.
I don't make fool's prayers like these: "Oh, may that corner
adjacent to my field, spoiling its shape, be added to it."
"Oh, may my luck lead me to a pot of money! It happened once, 10
to a plowman who bought a field with what he found there
and plowed it for himself. Hercules liked him, that's why
he got rich." I like what I have and offer you this prayer:
Fatten the flocks of which I'm master and all else except
my head and be, as you've always been, my great protector. 15
Now that I've left the city for this hilly citadel,
my satire, my humble verse, will show why I prefer it here.
Here are no corrupting forces, and no south wind of lead
and fatal Fall[3] to make the gloomy funeral goddess rich.
Father of the morning or Janus, if you prefer that name, 20
to whom men consecrate their early tasks each day
(for so the gods decreed), I'll start my song with you.
In Rome you rush me into court to speak well of a friend. "Move!
Someone might be quicker than you to do his duty. Run!"
Whether the north wind is razoring the land or winter, 25
deepening, shortens the circle of each day, still I go.
Having spoken, loud and clear, what may hurt me later,
I'm forced to fight the crowds, bumping slower walkers.
One jerk gets angry and yells out: "What the hell, you nut,
what's your problem? Go ahead, knock everybody down! 30
Getting back to Maecenas is all you think about."
Those words are sweet; I don't deny that. But the Esquiline![4]

---

1. Horace's farm in the Sabine country of Italy, presented to him by Maecenas three or four years previously.
2. Mercury, god of luck and lucre.
3. The sirocco, a south wind from Africa, causes a strange, leaden sense of oppression. Autumn, the proverbial season of ill health for the Romans, apparently did not affect Horace in the Sabine hill country.
4. The Esquiline Hill, where Maecenas' private gardens were located. It is called "dreary" because it had formerly been a burial ground. Cf. *S*.I.8.7 and note.

It's dreary, and the moment I arrive a hundred chores
that don't concern me invade my head from every side. "By seven
Roscius wants to see you at the sacred wall, tomorrow."   35
"Something new's come up of great importance to all clerks;
the guild[5] wants you back today, Quintus, don't forget."
"Get Maecenas to stamp these papers with his seal." I say,
"I'll try." "You can if you want," he adds, and he insists.
The seventh year, more like the eighth, has now flown past   40
since first Maecenas added me to the number of his friends,
to keep him company in the carriage when he traveled
and be his confidant for these remarks: "What time is it?"
"You think the Thracian Bantam can give Syrus a good fight?"
"If you don't dress warmly, this morning air can really bite."   45
These are safe state secrets for a leaky ear like mine.
Envy burdens our hero, as long as he's in town, each hour,
all day. After watching the games and playing on the Campus
with my friend, everyone calls me "Fortune's son."
A scary rumor moves from the Forum through the streets.   50
Each man I meet consults me: "Sir—I'm sure you know,
you're close to all the big shots—what about the Dacians?"
"I don't know." "There you go again, always making jokes."
"May the gods upend me if I've heard one whisper!"
"What about the vets? Will the farms that Caesar promised   55
be in Sicily, or will he offer them Italian land?"
Swearing I know nothing makes me wondered at, as if I alone,
among all men, am master of such deep, astounding silences.
My whole day is wasted like this, except for when I pray:
Oh, country home, when will I see you? And when drink in   60
from old books, from sleep, from the passing lazy hours,
forgetfulness of this troubled life I'm leading now?
When will the bean, Pythagoras's cousin,[6] be served me,
and vegetables that plain bacon fat will oil to my taste?
Ah, nights and dinners fit for gods! My friends and I   65
before the fire while I offer to my slaves, who won't be shushed,
what's left upon our plates. Here each guest is free
and can mix his wine the way he likes it, released
from silly rules, whether he can handle something strong
or gets happily lit on a blend that's mild. And then   70
a conversation starts, but not on others' farms and houses,
or how well or badly Mr. Charming dances; for our topics
we find more important: to be ignorant of them is wrong.
"What brings men happiness, virtue or much wealth?"
"Does a useful or a good man make the better friend?"   75
"What, exactly, does 'good' mean? What is the highest good?"
Here my neighbor, Cervius, tells grandmothers' tales,
with a purpose. If someone praises what Arellius has,

5. Horace himself had once been a clerk and was still a
member of their guild. Here Horace is addressed famil-
iarly by his praenomen and told about an upcoming
meeting of the guild.
6. The philosopher Pythagoras, who taught the doctrine of transmigration of souls, forbade his followers to
eat meat, for fear they might be eating friends or rela-

tives reincarnated as animals. In addition, he forbade
the eating of beans; by Horace's time, the reasons offered for this latter prohibition varied widely. Here
Horace humorously applies the doctrine of transmigration of souls to beans as well. See Pythagoras in
Glossary.

not knowing that wealth brings trouble, he starts in: "Once
a country mouse welcomed a city mouse into his home,   80
his barren cave, for the two of them had long been friends.
The host lived simply, without waste, but knew how to ease
his straitened soul in hospitality. You understand. And so,
he gladly gave his guest the best garbanzos and best oats,
he carried him raisins in his mouth and pieces of bacon,   85
all in vain. He tried various foods, but none could best
a taste that barely nibbled each, and with a haughty tooth.
The entire time the country mouse lay upon a bed of chaff
and ate plain spelt and darnel; the fancy stuff he served.
Finally the city mouse inquired: 'What's the fun, my friend,   90
of living here, camping on this steep and wooded ridge?
How can you prefer these savage woods to cities and to men?
Seize the road! Trust me, your pal! For nature gives
us earthly creatures mortal souls, and there's no escaping death
for anyone, large or small. That's why I say, old buddy,   95
live happily while you can with things that you enjoy;
live mindful of the shortness of your time.' Inspiring words,
and the hick, inspired, leaps gaily from his hole;
together they set off, eager to reach and then to creep
beneath the city's walls by dark. And so, as Night   100
lays claim to Heaven's center, each traveler stands
inside a palace of a house where rich red covers
tossed on ivory couches blaze out like flames
and great serving trays remain, relics of the evening,
the great feast, piled up in baskets by the table.   105
So, once he has his rural guest relaxed on purple cloth,
a napkin, the host rushes around like a bare-legged boy
and keeps the dishes coming, performs his duties
in true slavish style, tasting first all that he serves.
The other lies back, enjoys his role as festive diner,   110
as well as all the food; but suddenly a mighty clattering
crash of banging doors knocks both mice from their couches.
They skitter around the room in terror, then get more scared
and more confused as the great hall rings with echoing bays,
bellowed by Molossian hounds. The hayseed gasps, 'This life   115
I don't need, goodbye! My woods and cave will guard me
from all snares, and plain vetch will be my consolation.' "

7

Davus: It's me, the slave you've been talking at for years; and now I'd tell
you a thing or two, if I dared. *Horace:* Davus? *Dav:* Yes, Davus, your servant,
loyal and honest. Honest enough, that is. Not too good to live,
don't worry about that. *Hor:* Well, December's freedom month,[1]
since our ancestors wanted it that way, so be free. Speak.   5
Dav: Some men like being evil all the time and work hard at it,
but most just float, occasionally going right, as often
giving up and going wrong. Priscus often wore three rings,

---

1. The time of the Saturnalia. See *S.*II.3.5 and note.

and was sneered at, but sometimes he showed his left hand bare.
He lived an uneven life, changing his stripe[2] each hour;   10
on a whim he'd flee his fancy house and squat in dumps
in which a self-respecting freedman wouldn't be caught dead.
In Rome he chose an adulterer's life, in Athens
a scholar's. Every Vertumnus in heaven frowned upon his birth.
After Volanerius's high living had earned him gout,   15
which lamed his fingers, he rented a slave to gather up
his dice and replace them in their cup, a service
he paid for by the day. Since Volanerius was faithful
to the same old vice, he suffered less, enjoyed life more,
than someone straining on a leash alternately tight and loose.   20
Hor: What's the point of all this crap? And when, Forkbait,[3]
will you get there, today? *Dav:* You're the point. *Hor:* You're nuts! Why?
                                                        Dav: You praise
the life and customs of the good old days, but suppose a god
appeared right now to take you back? You'd instantly refuse.
You don't really believe that stuff you preach, or, anyway,   25
you're not too firm in its defense. Fact is, you're stuck
in your own sentimental slush and wish you weren't.
In Rome you want the country; away, my fickle farmer,
you praise the city to the skies. If not invited out
to dinner, you praise your salad, your good fortune,   30
and yourself, as if you never went away without being dragged,
all this because you lack a place to go. Then the summons
of Maecenas comes, quite late. An invitation! So you rush,
and bellow: "The torch! Bring it! Hurry! Are you all deaf?"
You jabber and sputter and have a fit, then you run.   35
Mulvius and your other leeches, spitting curses at you
that I can't repeat, go stomping off. "I admit," says Mulvius,
"I'm easily led by my belly, my nose pursues good smells.
I'm lazy, stupid, and—I don't deny the name—a pig.
But you're the same, and maybe worse. What makes you so free   40
to condemn me, as if you were any better, but hide
your crimes with pretty words?" You seem to be a bigger fool
than even I am, and I was very inexpensive. Take away
that scary face, and please control your hand and spleen
as I tell you what the doorman of Crispinus said to me.   45
A married lady's got hold of you, a whore's got Davus.
Which of us is worse, who more deserves the cross?
If my blood gets hot, with clothes off and the lamp lit,
she, it doesn't matter who, happily accepts my swollen meat,
or takes a shifting seat upon me, steed supine,   50
then sends me home with no scandal, and no worries
about someone handsomer or richer coming in her next.
When you've discarded all your signs of rank, the knight's ring,
the Roman toga, and go out on the town changed from a judge

2. Roman senators had a broad purple stripe on their tunics, knights had a narrow one.
3. The *furca*, or "fork," was an instrument of punishment in the form of a two-pronged fork, placed on the prisoner's neck while his hands were tied to the two ends. "Forkbait" was a term of vituperation usually reserved for slaves.

to lowly Dama,[4] hiding your anointed head beneath a hood, 55
aren't you really what you seem? You're nervous at the door,
then shake, as lust and panic take their turns within you.
What's the difference between an official flogging
or execution and the shame of being shut up in a chest,
hidden there by the erring lady's maid, where you lie 60
in a knot, knees joined to head? And doesn't the husband
of the faithless wife hold power justly over both of you,
but especially over you, the man? For she didn't change
her clothes and hide her rank, and isn't the main sinner.
She's just the woman, whom you frightened and misled. 65
Exit forked—you knew you would—and to the irate husband
goes the charge of all you have, your life, property, and name.
Ah, escaped? Well-scared, I hope, and well-taught to beware.
No, you want to be scared again; if you can set it up,
you'll risk death twice. Slave! Complete slave! No beast 70
freed from a trap is so perverse he'd go back in it.
"I'm no adulterer," you say. Well, by Hercules, I'm no thief!
Because if I stole the silver I'd get caught. Remove the risk,
and our wild natures would spring forward with no reins.
Are you really my master? You take orders too, many of them, 75
from men and from things, and three or four touches
with a freedom rod[5] will never end your servitude of fear.
Here's an equally important and related point: if
someone owned by a slave, as the law allows, is either
underslave or fellow slave, then which am I? Surely, 80
though you rule me, you've wrecked your life by serving others;
they lead you like a puppet jerked by handlers' strings.
So, who is free? The wise man, who can rule himself
and isn't scared of poverty, or death, or chains.
He can deny desire, spurn rewards. For he's strong 85
and wholly self-sufficient, like a polished sphere[6]:
nothing from outside stays fixed on his smooth hide.
Fortune tries to rush him, but she always breaks her leg.
Can you find one of his qualities in you? Your girl demands
five talents, and gives you hell: slams doors on you, 90
pours ice water on you, then lets you in. Free your neck
of that disgraceful yoke. "But I am free, I am." Oh, sure.
Not with that cruel driver, fiercely lashing at your soul
from underneath when you get tired, forcing you against your will.
Also, when you're in a stupor, "appreciating" a Pausias, 95
and I'm on tiptoe staring at Fulvius and Rutuba
or Pacideianus[7] in red chalk or charcoal, why am I
the guilty one? In those pictures you see gladiators
really fighting, swinging and ducking, waving weapons.
But I'm "that lazy staller, Davus," and what are you? 100
"That keen and clever judge of fine old works of art."

---

4. See *S.I.6.38* and note.
5. In the formal manumission ceremony before the praetor, the slave was touched with the lictor's rod.
6. According to the Stoics, the sage is self-contained,

needing no externals, and thus is like the perfect and complete sphere of the cosmos.
7. Gladiators pictured in advertisements.

I'm a pancake sniffer and so, despised. But do you,
with your great virtue, copious soul, decline the richest foods?
Yielding to my belly will get me into trouble, but how?
It gets me whipped across the back. Are you punished less   105
just because your favorite foods are rare and costly?
For a meal attacked without restraint turns sour,
and feet betrayed by wine won't bear a rotted frame.
How criminal is a slave who takes a bath brush, to trade
for grapes after his work? And isn't anyone who sells   110
his land to serve his gut just a trifle slavish? Moreover,
you can't be alone one hour, and all your leisure time
you waste. You flee yourself, like a runaway slave,
seeking now in wine, now sleep, a deliverance from care.
No good. You flee, but that dark companion keeps pursuing.   115
Hor: Where's a stone for me? *Dav:* What? *Hor:* Any arrows around here?
Dav: Either he's gone mad or he's making a poem. *Hor:* Move faster,
get going, or be field hand number 9 out on my Sabine farm.

8

Horace: Did you enjoy dinner with Nasidienus, the rich man?
I wanted you for my guest yesterday, but learned you were
with him, drinking since noon. *Fundanius:* Right, and never in my life
enjoyed a dinner more. *Hor:* If you have the time, please tell me
what dish came first, to appease your snarling stomach?   5
Fun: A Lucanian boar, killed, said the father of the feast,
as the south wind gently blew. Bitter things came with it,
stuff that can invigorate bored bellies: two kinds of radish,·
lettuce, skirret root, fish-pickle, Coan tartar lees.[1]
When that was all removed, a bare-legged slave came in   10
to wipe the table with a purple cloth, and another boy
to gather up the errant crumbs and any other things
which might annoy the guests. Then black Hydaspes brought
Caecuban wine—he marched along, like a Greek maiden
bearing Ceres' gifts—and Alcon served us brine-free Chian.   15
The master said: "Maecenas, if Alban or Falernian wine
would suit you better than what's here, I've got both."
Hor: It's tough to be rich. But who had dinner with you,
Fundanius, that made it such a great event? I'm curious.
Fun: I had the first couch and Viscus Thurinus was next.   20
Then, if I recall, came Varius, and by Servilius Balatro
lay Vibidius; those two were shadows[2] that Maecenas brought.
The host was flanked by Nomentanus and by Porcius,
a joker whose special trick was gulping down whole cakes.
It was the job of Nomentanus to reveal all the secrets   25
on the table, pointing with his finger, but we masses
were still confused, eating birds, oysters, and fish
with flavors not at all resembling any food we knew.
This I understood as soon as Nasidienus served me livers,

---

1. See *S.*II.4.73 and note. Greek Coan wine ranked second only to that made at Chios.

2. Guests who were not invited in their own right but came with a man of higher station. Servilius and Vibidius were hangers-on of Maecenas.

turbot and flounder livers, which I'd never had before.   30
Next he told me why his sugar apples happened to be red:
they were picked beneath a waning moon. Why that matters,
ask him. Then Vibidius made this suggestion to Balatro:
"Let's get drunk and wreck his feast. Why die without revenge?"
So he asked for larger cups. Across our caterer's face   35
a pallor spread, for more than anything he was frightened
of big drinkers, hating either their loud and vulgar talk
or their palates' dullness when heated by the wine.
They emptied whole decanters into huge Allifan mugs,
Vibidius and Balatro did, and we all did the same,   40
all but the host's parasites, who let the bottle sit.
A lamprey was brought in, lying on a platter in a sea
of swimming prawns. "It was gravid when caught," observed
the master. "After spawning, the meat's not quite so good.
Here's the recipe for the sauce: Venafran olive oil,   45
the first pressing; the roe from Spanish mackerel;
wine aged five years, from this side of the water
(for the cooking—then pour in just Chian, no other).
After that, you add white pepper and a drop of vinegar,
altered issue of the fermented Methymnaean grape.   50
Then you boil, adding coleworts and tart elecampane,
as I first showed (though Curtillus, it's true, discovered
that the shells of unwashed urchins made the better brine)."
Just then the hangings overhead crashed down, ruining
the lamprey and bringing with them more black dust   55
than the north wind raises in Campania's fields.
We feared more damage, but when all seemed at last secure,
we looked around; Nasidienus put his head down on the table
crying as if his little son had died. He'd never have stopped
if not for Nomentanus, the philosopher, who helped his friend   60
by saying: "Ah, Fortune! What god more cruel to us than you?
You always like to play around with mankind's hopes!"
Varius could barely hold his laughter back, behind a cloth,
and then Balatro, who's so snotty about everything,
added this: "Such is the nature of life, thus it happens   65
that our reputations don't correspond to our hard work.
To treat me properly, you see, you must lie upon the rack,
tortured by so many problems: you can't burn the toast,
you don't dare serve a poorly seasoned sauce, and every slave
around the table must be well dressed and neatly combed.   70
Also, there's the unforeseen, hangings that collapse,
like those there, and slaves who trip and break the dishes.
But a party-giver's talent, like a general's, comes out
in case of trouble, lies hidden when the going's good."
Nasidienus answered: "Whatever you ask for in your prayers,   75
may the gods grant. You're a decent man and a fine guest."
He called for his slippers and went out. Can't you just see it?
All of us whispering on our couches and cupping our ears?
Hor: I can't think of any comedy I'd rather see, but please,

don't stop. What did you laugh at next? *Fun:* Then Vibidius   80
asked the slave if someone had broken the bottle too,
for they hadn't brought the wine he wanted; Balatro joined
in this routine, which we made our excuse for laughing,
until, Nasidienus, you returned. You looked better, ready
to correct erring nature with your art, and your slaves   85
carried to the table, laid upon a giant board, a crane
severed into parts and coated well with salt and crumbs,
the liver of a fig-fed, albino gander, and rabbit legs
torn from the trunk: that way they're daintier etc.
than if still connected to the rabbit. Next course   90
was boiled blackbird breasts served with de-assed doves,
quite a treat without the lecture that his lordship gave
about their causes and essential natures. In revenge, we fled
before we took one bite—as if all the food was tainted
by Canidia's breath, fouler than any snake's in Africa.   95

The Epistles

Book I

1

My very first Muse sang of you, as will my very last.
I did well and have a practice sword to prove it. Why then,
Maecenas, do you want this old gladiator back in school?[1]
I've grown older and my needs have changed. Veianius hangs
his blade on Hercules' door and hides out on a farm   5
rather than beg the crowd too often from the ring.
To my well-cleansed ear there comes a voice that says:
"Free your old horse while you still can; show wisdom,
or he'll fall at the finish, be laughed at, burst his lungs."
So now I lay my verses down, and all my other games,   10
to study what is true and good, totally involved in that.
I gather and accumulate supplies[2] that I'll soon use.
If you wonder who leads me, whose house I shelter in,
no master has my allegiance: I swore oaths to no one.
Wherever the wind takes me, there I'll feel at home.   15
Now I become active and plunge deep in civic waters
as true virtue's guardian and firm support,
now fall slyly back upon the words of Aristippus
and make things submit to me, not myself to things.
The night is long to lovers whose girls deceive them,   20
days are long to workingmen. The year goes at a lazy pace
for minor sons weighed down by mothers' harsh control.
As slowly pass for me the boring hours which delay
my hope and plan: to concentrate upon a task
equally helpful to the poor and those with money,   25
equally harmful to children and the old if they neglect it.
Even with my tyro's truths I can soothe and guide myself.
In sharpness of vision you're no match for Lynceus,
but you don't despise ointment if you have sore eyes;
and though you'll never match unbeaten Glycon's strength,   30
you guard yourself against attacks of crippling gout.
We advance part way even if we can't go further.
Avarice and vile lust may be burning in your heart,
but certain spells and magic sayings can reduce the pain
and along with that drive out almost all of the disease.   35
Ambition can bloat you, but this sorcery can heal.
Cleanse yourself, then read the formula three times.
Envious, wrathful, lazy, drunken men, lewd lovers too,
none is so thoroughly wild a beast he can't be tamed,
if only he'll lend for cultivation's sake an open ear.   40
Virtue begins with fleeing vice and wisdom starts

1. Horace likens himself to a successful old gladiator who has been awarded the wooden practice sword, the symbol of discharge from the school, or training camp, for gladiators.
2. Horace declines to write more lyric poetry in favor of pursuing philosophy eclectically, attaching himself to no formal school of thought (14–19). He believes that the rudiments of philosophy, even incompletely understood, can, like magic spells used against bodily disease, help to cure diseases of the spirit (33–40).

in being a fool no longer. When do your greatest fears,
going broke, a bad defeat at the polls, hurt you the most?
When you risk your life and happiness to avoid them.
A tireless trader, you rush to the Indies far away   45
in flight from poverty, crossing mountains, seas, and flames.
To stop caring about these things you gawk at and desire,
can't you listen to, learn from, and believe a wiser man?
What small-time wrestler on tour among the villages
would scorn the great Olympic crown if he could hope for,   50
could expect, the valued prize and never have to sweat?
Silver has less worth than gold, gold less than virtue.
"O citizens, citizens, before all else seek money first.
Money, then virtue." So the Janus[3] everywhere declares
from top to bottom, and young and old alike recite it,   55
slates and school bags slung over left shoulders.
You have brains, character, eloquence, and loyalty,
and a fortune a bit below four hundred grand:
you're trash. But in their games boys say "You'll be king
if you do right." Make this your barrier of bronze,   60
that no crime burdens you, no guilt has turned you pale.
Tell me, is the Roscian Law[4] better than the boys' law,
their song making you a king if only you do right,
and which the virile Curii and Camilli used to sing?
Who's the better guide, someone who says, "Money, get money.   65
Rightly if you can; if not, any way you can, but get it,"
and earn a closer look at the teary plays of Pupius,
or an adviser[5] who tells you to defy proud fortune
by standing straight and free, who always helps you?
But if the Roman people should ever ask me why   70
I don't share their opinions as I do their colonnades
and pursue or run from what they themselves adore or hate,
I'll remember what the cautious fox told the sick lion
and answer: "Because these footprints make me afraid,
all of them going in towards you, none coming back out."   75
The beast has many heads. What should I follow and whom?
Some men like contracting with the government, others hunt
for rich old ladies they pursue with apples and with crusts,
or trap old gentlemen in snares to put in private zoos.
Many make secret loans and reap the interest. So,   80
you see that different things and crazes grip mankind;
but can any man keep liking one thing for one hour?
"Ah, shining Baiae! No bay more beautiful than you!"
If a rich man says this, lakes and seas will feel his love,
the impatient love of lords; then, when his corrupted fancy   85
delivers him its sacred sign, we hear "Tomorrow, Teanum!
Workmen, let's go!" His marriage bed[6] is in his hall?
Nothing, he'll say, but nothing, beats bachelorhood.

3. See S.II.3.19 and note.
4. L. Roscius Otho, tribune of the people in 68 B.C., carried a law which reserved the first fourteen rows of theater seats behind the orchestra for the knights. Since the knights generally were wealthy merchants, the Roscian Law embodied the undue public respect given to the wealthy.
5. The moral philosopher or, perhaps, Philosophy personified.
6. In a married man's household, a bed was placed in the hall and dedicated to the Genius, or guardian spirit.

No bed? He'll swear that only married men have fun.
What knot can I use to hold this Proteus, this shifter?   90
Poor men are no better off, changing garrets, beds,
baths, and barbers, going sailing on their hired boats
and getting just as sick as rich men on their own triremes.
After an unbalanced barber has given me a trimming,
if we meet, you laugh; if my ragged underclothes   95
peek out beneath a brand new tunic or if my toga's crooked,
you laugh. But suppose my reason is warring with itself,
scorns what it wanted, wants back what it just scorned,
foams like the surf, clashes with the rhythm of all life,
tears down and then builds up, turns squares to circles?   100
My madness is nothing strange, you think, and don't laugh
and don't suggest a doctor or a keeper chosen by the state,
although you take a guardian's interest in my life
and get angry if you see a ragged fingernail on me,
the friend who depends on you and on your good advice.   105
A final word: the wise man stands just below Jove: wealthy,
free, famous, handsome; a king, in other words, of kings.
Above all, he's sane (unless, that is, he has a cold).[7]

2

Lollius, my friend, the poet of the Trojan War,[1]
whom you declaim in Rome and I read over in Praeneste,
is both clearer and fuller on beauty and ugliness,
on good sense and nonsense, than Chrysippus and Crantor.
And if you have the time to listen, I'll tell you why.   5
The story, in describing how, because of Paris's romance,
Greeks and barbarians came to clash in prolonged war,
shows us the fiery passions of foolish kings and men.
Antenor suggests they stop the war by cutting out its root.
What does Paris think? A secure reign and happy life   10
he won't have forced on him. Nestor hastens to make peace
between the feuding sons of Peleus and Atreus.[2]
Love inflames the one, and anger both, to mutual heat.
Whatever actions their mad kings take, the Achaeans pay.
Treachery, fraud, impiety, lustfulness, and rage—   15
you find all these inside Troy's walls and outside too.
However, what bravery and intellect can do
is taught by the useful example of Ulysses,
the resourceful leader who took Troy and saw so many
of the cities and the ways of men; on the open sea,   20
scheming his return and his comrades,' he suffered much,
but he wouldn't sink beneath the hostile waves.
You know about the Sirens' song and Circe's potion[3]:
had he drunk like the others, so stupid and so eager,

---

7. For the Stoic paradoxes playfully mentioned here, see *S.*I.3.123 and note, *S.*II.3 and initial note.

1. The Greek poet Homer, whose epic the *Iliad* relates events in the tenth year of the Greek siege of Troy. His *Odyssey* tells of the Greek hero Odysseus' attempts to return home following the sack of Troy. Both epics were often read by the ancients as sources of moral wisdom.

2. Achilles, the son of Peleus, and Agamemnon, the son of Atreus, quarreled over the possession of the captive woman Chryseis. The bitter anger of Achilles over this feud is the announced subject of Homer's *Iliad*.

3. Circe, an enchantress living on the fabulous island Aeaea, turned Odysseus' men into swine by means of a potion (*Odyssey* X.230 ff.).

ruled by a whore, he'd have become both brainless   25
and foul, like a dirty dog or a pig who loves the mud.
We're mere numbers, simple eaters of earth's substance,
we are Penelope's wasteful suitors and Alcinous's
young men,[4] indecently busy at grooming their hides.
A good life to them meant snoozing until afternoon,   30
enjoying a lazy sleep, lulled by a cithara.
Robbers jump out of bed at night to kill a man;
can't you wake up to save yourself? Start running now,
when you're well, or you'll get sick and have to run.[5]
If you don't demand books and a lamp before day, if you   35
don't direct your thoughts to study and important things,
envy or lust will torment you and never let you sleep.
You quickly remove something from your eye that hurts it:
if rot is eating at your soul, why postpone the cure a year?
Once you start, it's nearly done. Be brave and wise: 40
Begin. Any man delaying when he could be living right
is like the hayseed who waits for the river to stop:
it flows and flows—in fact, it rushes—forever.
Men always desire money, wives who'll give them sons
and dowries, untamed land to conquer with the plow,   45
but anyone who has enough should want no more.
No house and farm, no heap of copper and gold
can drive a fever from its owner's weakened flesh
or his worries from his soul. He must be well
if he wants good use from everything he's gathered.   50
A man who desires or fears enjoys his goods as much
as a sore-eyed man likes art, a man with gout
fine shoes, someone with wax-plugged ears a cithara.
Anything you pour into a dirty pot gets spoiled.
Don't live for pleasure: its price is sorrow and pain.   55
Greedy men are always poor: set limits to desire.
Those who envy others grow thin despite vast wealth.
Envy—Sicilian tyrants could never have contrived
a better torture. Any man who can't control his rage
will wish undone what his emotions made him do   60
when, filled with vengeful wrath, he rushed to violence.
Anger, no matter how brief, is madness. Rule your passions
or they'll rule you; manage them with reins or with a leash.
A skillful trainer with a colt can teach it to obey
and take the path its rider wants. A young hunting dog   65
barking at a stuffed deer in his yard prepares for service
later in the woods. Now is the time to drink wise words
into your young and open heart; take instruction now
from your betters. A bouquet settling in a new-made jar
will long remain there. But if you delay or rush ahead,   70
I'll neither hang around and wait nor run to catch you.

---

4. Alcinous was king of the Phaeacians, who lived in ease and luxury on the mythical island of Scheria. He entertained the shipwrecked Odysseus.

5. Running was one form of exercise supposed to relieve dropsy.

3

To Julius Florus:
                    I'd like to know where on the earth
Tiberius, the Emperor's stepson,[1] is now soldiering?
Is your campaign delayed in Thrace, near ice-bound Hebrus,
or near the strait which runs along between the towers,[2]
or somewhere among the fruitful Asian hills and plains?   5
What is your staff of poets doing? That interests me too.
Who has chosen to write about Augustus and his deeds,
to spread his fame in war and peace throughout the future?
How's Titius? I'm sure he'll soon be big in Rome,
for he's not afraid to drink from Pindar's fountain   10
and bravely ignores more accessible pools and streams.
Is he well? Does he remember me? Is he following his Muse,
by fitting Theban rhythms to the Latin lyre,
or raging and blowing away, trying to be tragic?
What about Celsus? Warned once, he should be often warned   15
to write his own work and not borrow bits from every poem
Apollo adds to his library[3] on the Palatine Hill.
If somehow those birds returned and claimed their feathers,
then laughter would greet our little crow, his stolen plumes
all stripped away. And tell me, Florus, what about you?   20
What flowers do you buzz around? Your talent isn't slight,
nor is it left uncultivated and shamefully unkempt.
You may be sharpening your skill at legal rhetoric
or learning how to counsel clients or writing a poem—
no matter what, you'll get the first place ivy. But if   25
you could strip care's cold dressings from your soul,
you'd go where heaven's wisdom would take you, on a task,
a mission, that shouldn't be postponed by great or small
if they want to be respected by their country and themselves.
When writing back, you might inform me if your liking   30
for Munatius is as great as he deserves. Or, ill-stitched
the first time, is your friendship torn again? But listen:
whether it's hot blood or inexperience that plagues you,
you young colts with unbowed necks, wherever you are,
both of you too fine to break a brothers' pact,   35
I'm fattening a calf to sacrifice when both of you return.

4

Tibullus, plain-spoken judge of my plain satires,
what could you be doing now out on your Pedan land?[1]

---

1. Tiberius Claudius Nero, the son of Augustus' wife
Livia by a former marriage. He was destined to be
adopted by Augustus in A.D. 3 and to succeed him as
emperor in A.D. 14. In 20 B.C. Tiberius was sent to
Asia Minor to place Tigranes II on the Armenian throne
after the assassination of Artaxias II. His considerable
retinue included young men of literary aspirations, such
as Julius Florus; the young Roman poet Titius; Celsus
Albinovanus, Tiberius' friend and personal secretary;
and Munatius, whose father, L. Munatius Plancus, was
consul in 42 B.C.
2. The towers of the lovers Hero and Leander at Sestos

and Abydos, on opposite shores of the Hellespont.
Leander fell in love with Hero, a priestess of Aphrodite
at Sestos, and used to swim the strait nightly to see her.
One night a storm put out the tower-light by which she
guided him, and he drowned; grief-stricken, she threw
herself into the Hellespont.
3. The public library, created by Octavian in 28 B.C.
and located in the temple of Apollo on the Palatine Hill
in Rome.
1. Tibullus owned a villa near the Latian town of
Pedum, not far from Horace's Sabine estate.

Writing better things than Cassius of Parma used to?
Or walking quietly through the woods, keeping healthy,
intent on whatever thoughts concern the good and wise?   5
You always had a good heart, and the gods gave you
beauty and wealth and the gift of enjoying yourself.
What else could any nurse want for a sweet baby,
clever and able to express what he felt, who would have
charm, a good name, and health, all in full measure,   10
and a comfortable life with an adequate supply of cash?
Among men's cares and hopes, their fears and rages,
count as your last each morning that illuminates the sky:
then the next day, unhoped for, will always please you.
Come and see me, your fat, sleek friend with the shiny hide,   15
a pig from Epicurus's herd, if you ever want a laugh.

5

If you don't mind lying on an unstylish couch
and don't hate plain vegetables served on cheap plates,
come tonight, Torquatus, at sunset. I'll be waiting.
Expect wine from Taurus's second term,[1] bottled
in swampy Minturnae and in Petrinum near Sinuessa.   5
If you have any better, send it, or accept my choice.
The servants have cleaned the house, it's tidy for you.
Forget men's slight hopes and the trouble money brings,
forget the Moschus case. Tomorrow is Caesar's birthday,
making it legal to sleep late; and so, without a penalty,   10
we can prolong this summer night with pleasant talk.
What good is my money if I don't allow myself to spend?
Someone who lives a barren life, in saving for his heirs,
is nearly mad. I'm going to drink and scatter flowers,
and if you think my judgment isn't sound, so be it.   15
What can't a night of drinking do? It lets secrets out,
makes us see our hopes fulfilled, turns cowards to fighers,
lifts cares away from burdened souls, teaches new arts.
There's no one a few drinks can't make eloquent,
no one so ensnared by poverty they can't set free.   20
I accept certain chores without objection, as properly
the host's: to let no grimy cloth or dirty napkin
cause wrinkled noses; to offer you no plate or tankard
in which you fail to see your face; to invite real friends
who won't carry what we say outside; to have equal   25
meet equal. I'll get Butra and Septicius for you,
and Sabinus, but he might have another date by now,
or a girl he'd rather see. There's room for a few shadows,[2]
but if a party's crowded the people smell like goats.
Say how many you're bringing. Then forget the law   30
and duck out the back door; let your waiting client wait.

1. The wine had been bottled in 26 B.C., when Taurus   2. See *S*.II.8.22 and note.
was consul for the second time, with Augustus.

6

Numicius, never be astonished; that's really the one
and only way to find happiness and keep it.
The sun in the sky, the stars, the constant motion
of the seasons leave some observers free of fear.[1]
Tell me your opinion of the treasures of the earth   5
and of the sea, enriching Arabs and Indians far away,
of the empty cheers and titles that Roman voters give.
How do you regard these things, how feel and speak?
Anyone who fears their opposites will be astonished too,
as much as one desiring them: both men get shaken up,   10
any sudden change of fortune makes both men panic.
Why distinguish joy and grief, desire and fear
in anyone, faced with worse or better than he hoped,
who just stands and stares, numb in body and in brain?
Let wise men be called insane and the just unjust   15
if they too hotly pursue virtue: even that has limits.
Go on, gawk at silver work and old marble, at bronzes
and other pretty things, goggle at jewels and purple cloth,
be thrilled if a thousand eyes have seen you speak.
Get to the Forum[2] early and don't go home till dark,   20
for Mutus might reap more grain from the fields he got
by marriage—how disgusting: his origins are low.
Then you'd have to admire him, not the other way around.
Whatever lies beneath the earth time will bring to light,
and hide and bury all that glitters now. Famous as you are,   25
the Colonnade and Appian Way will see the last of you,
and down you'll go where Numa and Ancus went before.
If disease attacks your chest or kidneys, get medicine
to drive it out. You want to live right? Who doesn't?
If nothing but virtue can do it, be strong, give up   30
your pleasures, get busy. Or do you consider virtue words
and a sacred grove mere wood? Watch out. You may be second
into port and stuck with goods from Bithynia or Cibyra.
Heap up a thousand talents, then as much again; to that sum
add a third thousand, and a fourth to make the pile square.   35
I know, a wife with a dowry, good credit, friends,
family, and looks are all Queen Money's gifts: a man
with money gets blessed twice, by Venus and Suadela.
The Cappadocian king is rich in slaves, short on cash;
don't let that happen to you. Once, they say, Lucullus   40
was asked to give a hundred capes for a special play.
"How can I find so many?" he said. "Well, I'll look, and send
whatever I have." Then he wrote he'd found five thousand
scattered through his house; they could have all or some.
Only a poor man's house lacks much that isn't needed,   45

1. While the workings of the universe were looked upon by the ignorant as marvelous and fearful, philosophers such as the Epicureans or Pythagoreans were able to look upon the cosmos with tranquillity, not dread.
2. To do business.

which its owner doesn't know exists, to profit thieves. So,
if wealth alone can find and keep your happiness,
always be the first to seek it, the last to quit.
But if happiness is guaranteed by influence and rank,
buy a slave who can tell you people's names and nudge you   50
to extend your hand, while giving you the facts that count:
"That one's an important Fabian, the other a big Veline.[3]
This man here can make anyone a consul, or, if angered,
can take the ivory chair[4] away." "Father," "Brother,"—use
the word that fits the age and slickly adopt each man you meet.   55
If good eating means good living, then go out at dawn
and follow your nose, go hunting and fishing as once
Gargilius did: he ordered his slaves to carry nets
and spears into the Forum, full of people in the morning.
There, as everybody watched, one mule out of all his train   60
hauled off a purchased boar. Stuffed with undigested food,
we take our baths, forgetting what is right and what is not;
we're morally disfranchised, like Ithakan Ulysses' rotten crew[5]
to whom their country mattered less than did forbidden joy.
If, as Mimnermus likes to think, without love and games   65
nothing can give pleasure, spend your life in love and games.
Well, good luck. If you have advice more helpful than mine,
be open and share it. If not, use mine along with me.

7

I promised you I'd spend a week in the country.
I lied. I've been away all August.[1] But if you
want me strong and healthy, give me now, Maecenas,
the same consideration you give me when I'm sick,
for in Rome I'd be sick. The heat there and the early figs[2]   5
make the undertaker, with his black-robed crew, a wealthy man.
Mothers and fathers turn pale fearing for their children,
and social obligations joined with petty public tasks
cause fevers to rise and wills to be unsealed and read.
But later, when the snows of winter lie on Alba's farms,   10
I'll go to the coast to rest and read where it's quiet.
My friend, you'll see your poet again—provided
you want to—with the warm winds and first swallow.
You made me rich, but not the way a southern farmer
forces pears upon a guest. "Great pears! Eat more of them!"   15
"I'm full already." "Then take some with you." "No, but thanks."
"They're terrific for presents: surprise the kids!"
"I'm as grateful as if you'd loaded me with pears."
"Do what you want. Today the pigs will eat what's left."
A wasteful fool gives others what he disdains and hates,   20

3. Names of Roman tribes and, therefore, of regular
voting precincts.

4. The ivory curule chair was the privilege of the senior
magistrates.

5. Because Odysseus' (Ulysses') crew self-indulgently
feasted upon the forbidden Cattle of the Sun, they and
their ship were utterly destroyed by a storm sent by

Zeus. Only Odysseus, who did not eat of the cattle, was
spared.

1. The proverbial season of intolerable heat and illness
for the citizens of Rome.

2. The first figs of the season, which ripened in late
August, were considered bad for one's health.

and from such a sowing forever reaps ingratitude.
A wise, good man helps those worth helping and knows
the difference between a useful and a useless gift.
I'll show my thanks with honest praise for honest merit.
But if you never want me leaving you, then get me back   25
my healthy lungs, the black hair which draped my brow,
my old light talk and easy laughter and with them
the drunken tears I wept with impudent Cinara left.
Once a skinny little fox crawled into a bin of grain,
through a tiny chink; after having fed, it tried   30
to push itself back out again, but was too chubby.
A weasel was there and said: "If you want to escape,
you must go out that narrow hole as thin as you came in."
I can make that moral mine and give back all I have;
I don't praise the slumbers of the poor while overeating,   35
and I wouldn't trade my quiet freedom for Arabian wealth.
You've often praised my simple life (and "king" and "father"
are my words for you, whether you're there to hear or not).
See if I can't cheerfully return all that you gave me.
Enduring Ulysses' son, Telemachus,[3] spoke rather well: 40
"My land in Ithaca wasn't made for horses: it neither
stretches out in level plains nor bears abundant grass.
So, Menelaus, I return your gifts, which suit you better."
Little things suit little men: great Rome isn't my place
these days, but slow Tibur is, and peaceful Tarentum.   45
Philippus the famous lawyer, sharp and aggressive,
was walking back from court about one, complaining—
he wasn't young—about the distance from the Forum
to his home[4] when (the story says) he saw a man,
already shaved, in a cool and empty barbershop,   50
calmly using a small knife to clean his nails himself.
"Demetrius," (a slave, always quick to follow the orders
of Philippus), "go, find out that man's address, his name,
his rank, and who his father is or, perhaps, his patron."
He returned to say that the man was Volteius Mena,   55
an auctioneer with a small income and clean record, known
both to work and to relax, when proper, to earn and spend.
His pleasures were his unimportant friends, the house
he'd bought, the games and, after work, the Campus.[5]
"I'd like to verify your words by meeting their source: ask   60
the man to dinner." But Mena couldn't believe the invitation;
he just stared, that's all, and finally said, "No thanks."
"He turned *me* down!" "He did, the clown; what disrespect!
Or maybe he was scared." The next day Philippus saw Mena
on the job, selling junk to poor men dressed for work,   65
and got his hello in first. Mena made a few excuses:
For one thing, his occupation and its requirements

---

3. A paraphrase of *Odyssey* IV.601–608, in which
Telemachus politely refuses the chariot and team of
horses offered as a gift by Menelaus, King of Sparta.
4. The fashionable quarter where Philippus lived was
actually not far from the Forum, but the uphill approach
seemed like a long distance to the old man.
5. He watched the games; he exercised on the Campus.

didn't let him make morning calls,[6] and also, just then,
he hadn't seen him coming. "Consider yourself excused,
if today you come to dinner." "Why not?" "All right,   70
see you after three; now, get to work, make your money."
So he came to dinner, and he talked without restraint
until he left. He was often seen there after that
within the social swim—but headed for a hidden hook.
A morning client and a mealtime regular, he was asked,   75
at the Latin Festival, to visit the estate near town.
Drawn in a cart by Gallic ponies, he never stopped his praise
of the Sabine land and sky. Philippus saw and was amused.
Then, trying to relax and laugh whenever he could,
he gave Mena 7,000 sesterees, with a promised loan   80
of 7,000 more, and persuaded him to buy a little farm.
He bought it. I won't bother you with all the details,
just enough. The city man turned hick: he jabbered ceaselessly
of vines and furrows, he industriously pruned his elms,
he almost died of overwork, and greed aged him fast.   85
Then his sheep were all stolen and his goats all died,
his crops disappointed him, and he wore the ox out plowing.
These blows broke Mena down until, at last, one midnight,
he grabbed a nag and rode to Philippus in a fury.
As soon as Philippus saw him, all scruffy and uncared for,   90
he said, "Volteius, I think you're too hard a worker,
too diligent." "Patron," Mena answered, " 'miserable'
describes me best, if you're looking for the proper word.
By your Genius and honor, by your household gods,
I beg and I beseech you: give me back the life I had."   95
So any man who sees how greatly what he's given up
surpasses what he aimed at should return to what he had.
It's always best to measure yourself by a standard that fits you.

8

"Joy and great success to Celsus Albinovanus"—Muse,
send this wish to Tiberius's friend and secretary.[1]
If he asks what I'm doing, say, "Making fine promises,
but not living well." Say I'm depressed although no hail
has bruised my vines or hot weather scorched my olives,   5
and I'm not fretting about sick cows in some far pasture.
The problem is my mind, weaker than any bodily part,
for I won't learn about or listen to what might improve me.
I'm offended by truthful doctors and angry with my friends
who strike me as too eager to correct my fatal funk.   10
I seek what injures me, flee what I think may help.
The wind blows me: in Rome I love Tibur, in Tibur Rome.
Then ask how Celsus is, how he's managing his duties and himself,

---

6. In the Roman client-patron relationship, the client
might receive food, money, or legal assistance in return
for helping his patron in private and political life; in
addition, the client was expected to make a daily morning visit to his patron. Although Mena had declined
Philippus' dinner invitation, courtesy demanded that he
acknowledge Philippus' attentions by paying his re-
spects the next morning.

1. Horace's young friend Celsus was one of the retinue
accompanying Tiberius on his mission to the East in 20
B.C. See *E.I.3* and initial note.

and if he's won the favor of his young chief and the staff.
If he says he's doing well, tell him you're delighted,   15
but remember to let these words fall on his ears: "Celsus,
we'll endure you as well as you endure good fortune."

9

Hail Tiberius[1]: Septimius, surely the only man alive
who thinks I greatly matter to you, has asked, has begged,
me (of all people) to praise and recommend him to you
as a possible friend, high though your standards are.
He believes I have the honor of knowing you quite well,   5
that I have more power than I ever thought I had.
Of course I asked him again and again not to insist,
but I worried that he'd think I was knocking myself,
pretending I was useless, to save myself the trouble.
So, to escape the stigma of a major crime, I've sunk   10
to this, this blunt, big city pitch. But if you approve
the way I put modesty aside to meet a friend's request,
enroll him in your company, believe him strong and good.

10

To Fuscus, who loves the city, go wishes for his health
from a lover of the land. On that single point
we're far apart, on all the rest we're almost twins,
spiritual brothers with a shared disdain for certain things.
We nod together like a pair of old and friendly doves.   5
You're settled in your nest, I praise the idyllic country,
its little brooks, the rocks with mossy coats, the glades.
What more can I say? I'm alive, royally alive, when free
of what you all adore and raise up as high as heaven.
Like a slave who's sick of cake and runs away,   10
I prefer plain bread as better food than sweetened things.
If it's right to live the way that's natural for you,
first discover a good site, then construct your house.
Do you know of any place better than the blessed country,
where the winters are milder, where a gentler wind   15
soothes the angry Dog and swiftly-circling Lion,[1]
furious when he's pinked by the arrows of the sun,
where care, envious of sound sleep, disturbs it less?
Do Libyan marble floors look or smell better than grass?
Does purer water gush from pipes of lead in city streets   20
than that which flows and sings down slanting rural streams?
You know, people grow trees among their showy columns
and generally admire houses that overlook the fields.
Thrust nature out with a pitchfork—she'll come back,
and gradually she'll win, breaking through your fancy fakes. 25
A connoisseur who thinks a fleece stained purple
with our local lichens was tinted with Sidonian dye

---

1. This epistle was probably written just before
Tiberius' expedition to the east. See *E*.I.3 and initial
note.

1. The Dog-star rises on July 20 and becomes visible
about six days later; the sun enters the constellation of
Leo on July 23.

isn't hurt as badly or in such a vital spot
as someone who can't distinguish true from false.
A man who gets too happy when prosperity comes   30
trembles when it goes. Whatever you're wild about,
you hate to lose. Shun riches. Beneath a poor man's roof
life can surpass that led by kings and friends of kings.
A stag battled a horse for the best grass in a field
and kept on winning until the loser in that long war   35
approached a man to beg his help, and took the bit.
But when it had won the bloody clash and routed its foe,
it could neither shake out the bit nor shake off the rider.
Anyone so scared of poverty he'd rather lose his freedom
than his mines is such a fool he bears a rider, a master   40
he'll obey forever, since he never learned to live on little.
A fortune that doesn't fit its owner resembles shoes;
if too big, it makes him totter; if too small, it chafes.
Live wisely, Aristius; enjoy all that you have,
and don't let me escape if I'm caught grabbing more   45
than I have need of, or never turning from my work.
The money we amass will either rule or serve us;
we should lead it on a halter, rather than be led.
I dictate this behind Vacuna's crumbling shrine,[2]
wishing you were here, but otherwise quite happy.   50

11

How did Chios strike you, Bullatius, and famed Lesbos?
How did elegant Samos seem, and Croesus' royal Sardis?
Are Smyrna and Colophon better than we hear or worse?
Next to the Campus and the Tiber, do they all seem trivial?
Or is one of Attalus's cities everything you'd like?[1]   5
Or, tired of roads and sea, do you praise Lebedus[2] now?
You know about Lebedus, emptier than Gabii and
Fidenae, a village: still, I wouldn't mind staying there,
my friends forgotten, they having forgotten me,
to sit and watch as Neptune rages far from land.   10
But no traveler from Capua to Rome, rained on and smeared
with mud, would choose to stay forever in a roadside inn,
and no one in the cold would praise warm bakeries and baths
as the very best of places to lead a happy life.
Maybe the south wind rocked your ship in crossing,   15
but you wouldn't sell it on the Aegean's further side.
To a healthy mind Rhodes and lovely Mytilene[3] are worth

2. Vacuna was a local Sabine goddess. Horace plays
with a false etymology of her name, associating it with
vacuus, "idle."
1. Horace enumerates some exotic and frequently visited cities of Asia Minor. Chios, Samos, and Lesbos
were famous islands just off the coast of Asia Minor;
Smyrna and Colophon were Ionian cities, located on the
mainland near the coast. Further inland was Sardis, the
capital city of the Lydian king Croesus, famed for his
great wealth. The most important cities ruled by the line

of kings bearing the name Attalus were Pergamum,
Apollonia, and Thyatira, all some distance inland.
2. Unlike the illustrious places mentioned above, the
town of Lebedus, located on the coast between Smyrna
and Colophon, was small and fairly insignificant. The
Italian towns of Gabii and Fidenae had been important
in early Roman times, but by Horace's time were
merely deserted villages.
3. Rhodes was another celebrated island off Asia
Minor's coast; Mytilene was the capital city of Lesbos.

an overcoat at summer solstice, a jockstrap in the snow,
the Tiber when it's icy, in August a hot stove.
While I can, while fortune still looks upon me kindly,   20
I'll praise distant Samos, Chios, Rhodes—from Rome.
Bullatius, each hour that the gods make happy for you
gladly take; don't postpone happiness until next year,
so that, no matter where you've been, you'll say of life
that it was good. For if reason and discretion banish care,   25
rather than a view someplace of the spacious sea,
men who race across the sea change skies, not souls.
Our active idleness wears us out; with ships and chariots
we go looking for a decent life. What you seek is here,
it's at Ulubrae,[4] if you maintain a balance in your soul.   30

12

As the manager of Agrippa's land in Sicily, Iccius,
you'll gain as much there, if you take what you deserve,
as from anything that Jove could give you. Stop complaining.
No one is a pauper who has all the things he needs.
If your belly's good and your lungs and feet are healthy,   5
no royal treasure could add the slightest bit to yours.
You may have turned ascetic, for all I know, and live
on grass and nettles; you would stick to that diet
even if you fell in Midas's stream and turned gold.
That's so, either because money just can't affect you,   10
or because you think all things inferior to virtue.
We're amazed at Democritus, whose herds ate up his pasture
and his fields while his disembodied soul went flying free.
But you, although the itch for cash infects so many,
do not think small and do care about important questions[1]:   15
What keeps the sea in bounds? What controls the seasons?
Do the stars move in a pattern or wander where they like?
What obscures the moon, what brings its roundness back?
What does "concordant discord of things" mean, what do?
Is it Empedocles that's mad or Stertinius's point of view?   20
Anyway, whether you're murdering fish or leeks and onions,[2]
welcome Pompeius Grosphus, and if he wants something, gladly
give it; he'll only ask for what is suitable and right.
You can certainly afford to be friendly to a decent man.
Now I'll fill you in on Rome's affairs and get you current: 25
The Spaniards have yielded to Agrippa, the Armenians
to Tiberius, equally strong. Phraates, on his knees,
has accepted Caesar's rule and law. On Italy
Golden Plenty pours from laden horn abundant fruit.

---

4. A small, empty village of Latium, bordering on the
Pontine Marshes.

1. The following lines state some of the frequently
debated philosophical issues of Horace's day.

2. Pythagoras' belief in transmigration of souls led him
to forbid the eating of meat. Here Horace humorously
extends the doctrine to fish and vegetables. See
S.II.6.63 and note; Pythagoras (in Glossary).

13

To repeat again what I kept saying when you left,
Vinnius,[1] give these sealed volumes to Augustus
only if he's well and cheerful, and only if he asks.
Enthusiasm doesn't help: unless you want my little books
to be despised, don't try to sell me; restrain yourself.   5
And if the weight of all my paper chafes your back,
get rid of it somewhere before you reach the court;
that's better than dumbly smashing the load down there,
which would make you and your noble name of Ass ridiculous.
Exercise your muscles over the hills, rivers, and swamps;   10
then, when you've conquered them and reached your goal,
hold your burden right, not clamped beneath your arm
the way a yokel holds a lamb: it's just a few books.
Don't copy drunken Pyrrhia clutching her stolen wool
or a poor guest who has to carry his own cap and shoes.   15
And don't tell everyone what a sweat it was to bring
these odes, which may perhaps engage the eyes and ears
of Caesar. Now that I've made this lengthy prayer, push on.
Go, goodbye. Be careful not to fall and wreck your mission.

14

Steward of my woods and little farm which makes me whole,
which, though you despise it, shelters five families
whose five fathers regularly go to trade at Varia,
let's see if I've worked harder at weeding my own soul
than you my land: am I any better than my fields?   5
You know I'm kept in Rome by Lamia's concern and sorrow
(he mourns for his brother, laments a brother's death
and can't be cheered), but my heart and soul turn home.
I wish I could break the bars apart that block my way.
I say life in the country is happy; you say the city,   10
but any man who craves another's lot will hate his own.
We're both fools to blame a place, places are innocent.
The fault is in the soul, and it can't ever flee itself.
As my errand boy in town, you prayed in silence for a farm;
now, as farm steward, you want the city back, games and baths.   15
I'm consistent, as you know; it depresses me to go away,
and no matter what affair drags me to Rome, it isn't welcome.
Our enjoyments are different: that's the distinction
between the two of us. The place you consider hostile,
empty, and wild is lovely to someone like me, and I despise   20
what you think beautiful, whorehouses and greasy spoons.
These spur your urban dreams, I know. And you can't stand
my "patch of dirt that'll grow spice and pepper before grapes."
We don't even have a local saloon to serve you wine,
and without whores who play the flute, you can't dance   25
and do the stomp. Besides all that, you have to sweat

1. Horace has entrusted Vinnius with the task of bearing his recently finished Odes I–III to Augustus. Vinnius' cognomen was Asina, the Latin word for "ass"

(9); thus he is the appropriate "beast of burden" to
deliver Horace's "load."

on dirt no hoe has touched in years. Oxen get unhitched,
not you; you make them comfortable and serve their food.
When you want to loaf, a high river makes more work: in rains
your dikes of earth must teach it how to spare the fields.   30
Well then, why is there no harmony between us? Listen.
A fine toga once looked good on me; so did hair grease.
You know I made that greedy Cinara happy, without bribes,
and liked my clear Falernian at noon; but now what I enjoy
is eating simply and napping on the river's grassy bank.   35
There's no shame in having played, if you knew when to stop.
In the country no one looks sideways at my happiness,
slicing it down, or poisons it with hate from hidden fangs;
sure, they laugh—my neighbors—at me hauling rocks and dirt.
You want to go with the city slaves, eating city food,   40
you're eager to be one of them, but my clever groom,
who is, wishes he had your wood and herd and garden.
The ox wants a saddle, the lazy horse wants to plow.
I think each of us should do what he understands best.

15

Vala, what is winter like in Velia and Salernum?[1]
What are the people like? How about the roads? (For Baiae,
Dr. Musa says, won't help my health, and now, in fact,
they'll hate me there when I go to bathe in icy water
at winter's peak. Well, no one goes to see their myrtles,   5
or cares about their magic, muscle-soothing, sulphur baths;
naturally they're jealous and groan at the courageous sick
who bare their heads and bellies to the chilling springs
of Clusium or travel out to Gabii and the frozen fields.
So I have to visit someplace new and drive my horse   10
past all the usual stops. "Where to, horse? I'm not going
to Cumae or Baiae." But when I say that I'll sharply jerk
the left-hand rein, for a horse hears with its bridled mouth.)
Tell me which villages have more and better food,
and if they collect the rain for drinking or have wells   15
that don't go dry. I don't need to know about the wines.
On my farm I can endure or suffer any wine, I don't care;
but when I travel I bring good stuff, something smooth
to drive away my cares and make me rich in hope
as it flows up to my head, to give me eloquence,   20
to give me youth and a chance with Lucania's ladies.
Which area has more rabbits, which more wild boars?
Which stretch of surf conceals most urchins and most fish?
I'd like to be a fat Phaeacian[2] by the time I leave.
Send me a report: you're my unimpeachable source.   25
After Maenius blew his father's money having fun
(his mother's too), he gained a reputation as a parasite

1. Velia and Salernum were seaside towns south of
Naples, the former in the district of Lucania, the latter in
Campania. Baiae, also in Campania, was a seaside
resort famous for its hot sulphur baths. Located nearer

Rome were the cold water baths of Clusium in Etruria
and of Gabii in Latium.
2. See *E*.1.2.28 and note.

with class. He roved, never staying at one trough,
and, if he hadn't eaten, was the same to friend or foe:
he'd freely insult anyone, in any savage way he liked.   30
To the market he was a plague, a storm, a yawning gulf,
presenting to his greedy belly whatever he could find.
Sometimes, when those his dirt amused or frightened
would give him nothing, or not much, he'd gobble
by the plateful enough tripe and mutton for three bears.   35
On those occasions he was all for branding spendthrifts,
this prodigal reformed, with red-hot iron on the gut.
But if the same guy found richer plunder, he'd turn it all
to dust and ashes and, after that, declare: "By Hercules!
no wonder men eat up their fortunes! What could be better   40
than a juicy thrush, prettier than a fat sow's belly?"
I think I'm like him, praising sanity and moderation
when my funds are low; then I don't mind living cheap.
But if I have a chance for better, some luxury, I say
that only you, Vala, and your class know how to live,   45
in your beautiful country houses. That's real wealth.

16

Hail, Quinctius: Before you even ask about my farm—
whether I'm raising grain here or getting rich on olives,
or apples, or cattle, or on the vines trained on my elms—
I'll tell you about it, and its location, at some length.
In these mountains the one gap is my shadowed valley,   5
but the rising sun looks down upon its right-hand side
and when his chariot takes him off he warms the left.
You'd like the mild climate. And what if you could see
all my wild plums and berry bushes? And the oak and ilex
that delight my pigs with lots to eat and me with shade?   10
You might say Tarentum[1] had been brought here to bloom.
I have a spring so beautiful they named the river for it,
a spring as cold and clear as the winding Hebrus out in Thrace,
and its waters help sick stomachs, help aching heads.
It's a fine hiding-place, my paradise of a place   15
which keeps me healthy, believe me, all through September.[2]
Your life must be a good one if you try to earn your title:
"happy"— everyone in Rome has called you that for years.
But I worry that you'll trust another more than yourself,
or think you can be happy without being also wise and good.   20
If everybody praised your health and constant vigor,
but while eating you grew feverish, would you cover up
until the time your greasy hands began to shake?
Only an evil shame makes fools hide unhealed sores.
If someone speaking of your wars on land and sea   25
tried charming your receptive ears with words like these:
"Which of you wishes more good for the other, you or the people,
may Jove, who cares for both, keep forever in the dark,"

1. The luscious foliage of Tarentum, a city in Calabria,
was proverbial.

2. The hottest and unhealthiest season of the year in
Rome.

you'd know which man deserved that praise, only Augustus.
Though you might let yourself be called wise or perfect, 30
you'd act as if you hadn't heard, wouldn't you? "But surely
the title 'wise, good man' is one we all enjoy, you too."
And those granting it today can take it back tomorrow,
as they'll strip the fasces[3] from a consul found unworthy.
"Drop that," they say. "It's ours." I drop it and sadly leave. 35
If the same voice shouted "thief!," said I was a pervert,
claimed I'd drawn a noose around my father's neck,
would these false charges sting me, turn me red or white?
False honors please and empty slanders terrify
only liars and the sick. But what makes a man good? 40
Here's one who obeys the Senate, the statutes and the laws,
cuts through the legal tangles of many major cases,
secures property by his word, wins suits as a witness;
still, everyone inside his house and every neighbor
sees the filth he hides beneath his pretty, lying skin. 45
"I'm no thief or runaway." If my slave said that to me,
I'd tell him, "Here's your reward: I won't whip you."
"I haven't killed." "The crows won't eat you on the cross."
"I work, I'm good." We Sabines[4] are stern judges: plea denied.
For wolves have the sense to fear a covered pit, and hawks 50
a snare, and kite-fishes a dangling, hidden hook.
Decent people hate doing wrong because they love good;
you're just scared of punishment and won't take risks.
Given a chance to pull it off, you'd desecrate a shrine:
you steal beans, don't you? one bushel of my thousand. 55
The loss is trivial to me, but your act is still a crime.
One good man, known to all the Forum and the judges there,
when honoring the gods by offering them an ox or pig,
calls clearly out, "Janus, Father!" and, as clearly, "Apollo!"
Then, fearing to be heard, he moves his lips: "Lovely Laverna, 60
let me cover up. Let me seem pious and just to others.
Keep my crimes well-wrapped in night, my trickeries in fog."
How a miser is at all above a slave or one bit freer
when bent over picking at a penny stuck firmly to the curb
beats me. To desire like that is to fear, and no man 65
who lives in fear will I ever consider to be free.
A man has thrown his weapons down, deserted virtue's side,
if he runs after profit all the time and wallows in it.
However, when a captive can be sold, why kill him?
If he'll make a useful slave, let him herd and plow. 70
So, tell the merchant to sail across the winter waves
and bring back grain and other foods: he lowers prices.
A really wise, good man will dare to say: "Pentheus,[5]
King of Thebes, how will you humble me and give me pain?"
"I'll strip you of possessions." "Good. Take my herds, 75

3. Insignia of a consul. See *S*.I.6.97 and note.
4. Referring to the region of his farm.
5. Horace paraphrases Euripides' *Bacchae* 492–98, in which Pentheus, intent upon suppressing the Bacchic worship, threatens the god Dionysus, diguised as the Lydian leader of the Bacchantes. See *S*.II.3.303 and Agave (Glossary).

my silver, my couches. Those you may have." "I'll load you down
with cuffs and shackles, and your keeper will be cruel."
"God himself, when I desire it, will make me free." I think
he meant, "I shall die." Death is the finish line for all.

17

Scaeva,[1] you don't need anyone's advice; obviously you know
the right way to treat important people. Just the same,
listen to an old, unclever friend, eager to guide you.
Let a blind man lead the way. Give me a trial, and see:
perhaps you'll want to make some word of mine your own.   5
If peaceful quiet and late mornings spent in sleep
delight you, if dust and rumbling wheels and taverns
give you pain, go to Farentinum[2] and stay there.
For happiness comes not only to the rich, and no man
ever hated life because he lived and died obscure.   10
But if you want to benefit your friends and take it easy
on yourself as well, bring a good appetite to their good food.
Diogenes[3] once put Aristippus on the spot: "Just eat salad;
then you won't need kings." Aristippus said, "If you knew
how to handle kings, you could hate salad too." Tell me   15
whose words and life you recommend. No, since I'm older,
I'll tell you. Aristippus had the right idea, and this
is how he dodged the yapping cynic's thrusts: by saying to him,
"I leech for myself, you pimp for the crowd. My way's better
and pays better. To earn the good life my king provides   20
I do my job. You ask for peanuts, but, of course, depend
on those who throw them, despite your boasts of being free."
Anything fitted Aristippus, any condition, rank, or funds.
He aimed high but was generally content with what he had.
Not so his stern opponent, who wore a folded rag;   25
I'd be shocked if he could live in any other way.
Aristippus doesn't need to dress himself in purple,
but walks the crowded streets in whatever clothes he has;
let them be elegant or not, he'll play the proper part.
To Diogenes a shirt of fine Milesian cloth is worse   30
than a snake or rabid dog; he'll die of cold if you take
his rag away, so don't; let him live his stupid life.
To win great battles and show off captured foes at home
brings men nearly to Jove's chair and lets them touch the sky;
to have pleased such men is not the smallest honor I can name.   35
Not everyone can make it all the way to Corinth,[4]

1. This epistle teaches an important man's protégé how
to avoid sycophancy and preserve personal independence while maintaining equitable relations with his
patron. Of the Scaeva to whom it is addressed nothing is
known; Horace possibly chose the name, which means
"left-handed," as appropriate for a fictional figure he
wished to address, i.e., "Mr. Gauche."
2. A quiet country town.
3. This anecdote is a paraphrase of Diogenes Laertius
II.68. The Cynic philosopher Diogenes (ca. 412–323
B.C.) was washing some greens for his meager dinner

when Aristippus, the philosopher of Cyrenaic
hedonism, passed by. Diogenes aimed his gibe at Aristippus' taste for extravagance, which had led him to pay
court to Dionysius, the tyrant of Syracuse. Aristippus'
reply echoed his boasts elsewhere that philosophy gave
him the ability to remain at ease and uncorrupted in any
society; hence, for him, poverty was no sign of virtue.
4. The Greek proverb ran, "Not everyone may sail to
Corinth," meaning that not everyone may succeed in
achieving his goal.

so some, afraid to fail, won't try. That's natural.
And some get there. Have they acted as men really should?
That's the important question here. One man fears a load
which seems to overmatch his meager strength and meager spirit; 40
another lifts and carries it. Either virtue is an empty name,
or enterprising men should seek out their glory and reward.
Clients who don't tell their patrons how poor they are
get more than beggars do. And it's important to accept,
not grab. That's, the trick, the key, to this whole business. 45
"My sister has no dowry, my dear old mom is broke,
the farm's no good for crops, and we can't even sell it."
Why not just cry "Alms"? And since one beggar draws another,
yelling, "Hey, me too," the donation will be divided into bits.
If a crow could eat his meal in silence, he'd get more 50
when he found food, and with far less bitterness and fuss.
A companion riding to Brundisium or to beautiful Surrentum
who bitches about the bumps, the savage cold and rain,
or screams that someone broke his lock and took his cash
reminds me of a whore who thinks it's smart to whine 55
as often as she can about her stolen chains and garters.
Soon no one would believe her if she told the truth.
And no one who fell for it before will help a faker up
who says he's got a broken leg, even if he oozes tears
and swears by St. Osiris while he's speaking to the crowd: 60
"Me, trick you? Oh please, you monsters, help a cripple!"
But everyone just hoots and says, "Get another sucker."

18

I know, Lollius; you're honest, and fear if you became
a rich man's friend,[1] you might be called a parasite.
But a wife in white is as different from a whore
in brown as a real friend is from a parasitic fake.
The extreme opposed to flattery is almost worse, 5
that boorish, blunt, and out-of-place severity
which prides itself on hair cut short and dirty teeth
and expects plain rudeness to be called pure virtue.
Virtue lies between extremes, and far from either.
One man sinks too low, for at dinner he makes jokes 10
to please his patron, shivers when the great man frowns,
repeats his words, and passes on his wit before it dies.
You'd think he was a kid with a tyrant for a teacher
reciting lessons, or a bit player studying his lines.
The other will argue about goats, hairy or woolly? 15
He'll go to war for any stupid cause. "How can you
trust anyone more than me? I howl out whatever I like.
My honesty's not for sale, not another life could purchase me!"
What's the issue? Which of two actors has more skill,
which road is better when you're going to Brundisum. 20
A man who's lost his shirt on dice or on a woman,

---

1. Horace advises on the same subject as in *E*.I.17.

or overspent for vanity's sake on oils and clothes,
whom a driving hunger and a thirst for money grip,
or fear and shame of being poor, provokes his wealthy friend
(whose vices are often ten times worse) to hate, disgust.   25
Or, if he doesn't hate, he guides, like a dear old mother,
and urges the other man to be wiser and better than himself.
He comes near the truth in saying, "Me—you'd rival *me*?
My money lets me be a fool, but what have *you* got?
A cheap toga shows a prudent follower; stop trying   30
to be my competition." To ruin someone, Eutrapelus
would give him fancy clothes; with that kind of good luck,
a man will make his way of living match his style of dress
so that he'll sleep in the daytime, whore instead of work,
fatten the amounts he owes to others and, for a finish,   35
fight in the arena or drive a peddler's cart for pay.
Never pry into your great friend's private life,
and keep his secrets even if you're drunk or mad at him.
Don't praise what interests you or scorn what he enjoys,
or sit around composing poems when he prefers to hunt.   40
The friendship of twin brothers, of Amphion and
Zethus,[2] once broke up and wasn't mended until the lyre
stern Zethus didn't like was mute. We see that Amphion
let his brother have his way; respect your friend's position,
accept his light commands. So when he's going to the fields   45
and takes his dogs, his asses loaded with Aetolian nets,
get up, lay aside your melancholy, antisocial Muse
and earn your food by work as strenuous as his.
Roman men care about hunting; it gives them fame,
health, physical strength. And you're a natural,   50
faster than a dog at running, stronger than a boar.
Besides, at the manly art of handling weapons,
no one is better. You've heard how much the people cheer
when you battle on the Campus, and you fought bloodily
in Spain when just a youth, serving a commander[3] there   55
who now reclaims our battle flags from Parthia's shrines
and with Italy's strength controls all land not ours.
Suppose you don't feel friendly, it's wrong to leave.
Yes, I know you never lie or counterfeit emotions,
but you play around at times, out on your father's farm.   60
Opposing sides divide the rowboats, and Actium[4]
is fought again: you lead your slaves in battle order;
your brother is the foe, your pond the Adriatic, till
winged victory arrives, bringing one of you a leafy crown.
Anyone who thinks that you and he have common interests   65

2. Brothers who quarreled about the relative importance of the world of music and art versus the active life
of hunting and herding. Their rivalry was portrayed in
the *Antiope* of Euripides and in a later play of the same
name by the Roman poet Pacuvius.
3. Augustus led military campaigns in Spain during
27–25 B.C.; in 20 B.C. Augustus recovered through
negotiation the standards the Parthians had taken from
Crassus.
4. Lollius and his brother reenact on a miniature scale
the famous naval battle of Actium (31 B.C.), in which
Octavian defeated Antony.

will back you and praise your prowess with both thumbs.[5]
In case you need some more advice, I offer this:
Be careful what you say and to whom, about whom.
Run from a curious man; he'll love telling others.
Secrets that you trust to open ears won't be well kept,   70
and once a word escapes, it flies; you can't recall it.
Don't get heartburn over some little serving maid or boy
within the marble mansion of your much respected friend;
he may make that pretty boy or girl his final blessing,
a rather small one, or hurt your pride by saying no.   75
Before you introduce someone, study him over and over,
for if he soon goes wrong he'll bring disgrace to you.
But mistakes occur, and if a man whom you've brought in
is stained by guilt, don't you defend him: he tricked you.
Then you can help a real friend accused unjustly   80
and be the fortress that his loyalty deserves; besides,
when envy's teeth are gnawing him on every side,
how long can you expect to wait before you feel the bite?
If your neighbor's house is burning, your own is next;
for fires, if they're not put out, are apt to spread.   85
The inexperienced think it's fun to court the great,
those who know are cautious. When your ship is on the sea,
be alert, or be blown backward by a changing wind.
Gigglers are hated by the glum, the glum by jokers,
the lethargic by the quick, active men by sloths.   90
Drinkers who spend their nights soaking up Falernian
will hate you if you spurn a glass even if you swear
you're simply scared to run a fever after dark.
Keep your forehead free of clouds: a reserved person
seems to be concealing things, a quiet one to sneer.   95
In the little time left free, study the philosophers,
learn how to carry on with life and stay serene.
Must you be upset and torn by greed, that constant pauper?
Must fearing and craving things indifferent hurt you too?
Is it learning or nature that can make men good?   100
How can you worry less, how can you befriend yourself?
How is genuine peace conferred, by rank or tidy profits,
or a hidden path through life, a journey no one sees?
Each time cold Digentia[6] refreshes me, the river
that Mandela drinks, little village wrinkled by the cold,   105
can you guess my thoughts, my friend, believe my prayers?
"Let me keep whatever I have, or even less, but let me live
as many years as I have left, all that the gods allow.
Let me have a good supply of books and food all year,
and no fantastic hopes to keep me in suspense each hour."   110
But it's enough to pray to Jove for what he gives and takes.
May he grant life and means. A balanced soul I'll give myself.

5. Refers to the proverbial gesture with which the audience in the amphitheater expressed their approval; the
exact form of the gesture is unknown.

6. A small river which flowed past Horace's Sabine
villa and emptied into the Anio near the hill village of
Mandela.

191

Maecenas, learned friend, if you believe old Cratinus,
no poems can please for very long, or even live at all,
that water drinkers write. Since Bacchus thought them mad
he enrolled poets in his band, along with fauns and satyrs,
so the sweet Muses have often smelled winey in the morning.   5
By praising wine Homer is proved to have been a wino;
old father Ennius never leapt to sing of battle
without being drunk. "To the Forum and to Libo's busy well,[2]
consign all dries; I won't allow abstainers to sing."
From the day I delivered that decree poets haven't ceased   10
from drinking contests at night, stinking contests next day.
But if someone goes barefoot and wears a stern look
and cheap toga (custom made), and therefore looks like Cato,
do we find in him the character and qualities of Cato?
Iarbitas' envy of Timagenes' sharp tongue[3] destroyed him   15
when he worked so hard to be considered elegant and keen.
How misleading is a model with imitable flaws; if, let's say,
I had a pale face, poets would drink cumin and turn white.
O imitators, you slavish herd, how often have you raised
my laughter and my wrath with all your mad confusion!   20
I was the pioneer, walking free in unclaimed land,
not in another's tracks. Like any self-reliant man,
I brought a mob along behind me. I first showed Latium
Parian iambs, borrowing the rhythms and the vigor
of Archilochus, not his themes and words which killed Lycambes.[4]   25
And if you consider giving me lighter laurels
for being too timid to change his meter and technique,
man-souled Sappho shaped her Muse to the meter of Archilochus,
but, like Alcaeus, not to his subjects and his strophes.
No father was harried by Alcaeus, smeared with deadly verse,   30
no daughter strangled by a noose of scandalous song.
Before anyone else had tried, I brought Alcaeus here
upon my Latin lyre; I love bearing verse unknown before
to be read by citizens' eyes, cherished by their hands.
Then why do ungrateful readers praise and like at home   35
the things I write, unfairly sneer at them outside?
I don't hunt votes among our people, turned by every breeze,
by paying for their dinners and giving them used clothes.
I don't, after hearing other bards and taking my revenge,
stoop low to curry favor with the critics on their thrones.   40

1. This epistle assails Horace's imitators and answers the critics' charge that Horace's *Epodes* and *Odes* were mere imitations of Greek predecessors. Horace had creatively used the iambic poetry of Archilochus of Paros (fl. ca. 650 B.C.) as model and precedent for his own *Epodes;* the celebrated lyric poets of Lesbos, Sappho and Alcaeus (fl. ca. 600 B.C.), were a source of inspiration for Horace's *Odes*. Horace argues that he is not a servile imitator but a poet of the same school as these illustrious Greeks; he was no more an imitator of them than Sappho and Alcaeus themselves were imitators of Archilochus.

2. The well was in the Forum, where men gathered to conduct business.
3. Timagenes, a Greek rhetorician from Alexandria (fl. ca. 55 B.C.), who later came to Rome, was noted for his eloquence and extremely caustic wit. Iarbitas tried to imitate his rhetorical expertise but succeeded only in emulating his fault of acerbity.
4. Archilochus had been betrothed to Lycambes' daughter Neobule until Lycambes broke off the agreement. Archilochus leveled some of his bitterest and most scurrilous iambs at them.

Hence these tears.[5] "The crowded halls would be disgraced
to hear my little nothings read, as if they had real weight."
When I say this, they say, "Stop kidding: we know you keep
your work for just Jove's ears and think that poet's honey
flows from only you. You egotist!" At this I'm too afraid   45
to sneer: a rival with sharp fingernails might claw me.
So instead, I shout out, "Dirty trick!" and call for time.
Sport like this gives birth to furious strife and rage,
and rage in turn to savage feuds and murderous wars.

20

Book,[1] you have a yen, I see, for the Arcade and Vertumnus,
to sell there, at the Sosii's stand, your pumiced hide.
You despise the keys and seal and more modest types prefer;
exposed to few, you whine and long for common lovers.
You weren't raised for that, but go, down your chosen path;   5
once you're gone, you can't come back. "What came over me?
What did I want?" So you'll cry when someone injures you,
rolling you up small,[2] or a sated client puts you on the shelf.
Unless my rage at your mistake makes my prophecy go wild,
you'll be greatly prized in Rome till youth deserts you: 10
then, pawed over by the crowd and beginning to show signs
of getting dingy, you'll either feed illiterate moths,
or flee to Africa, or be sent, securely tied, to Spain.
Your guardian, his good advice all wasted, will laugh
like the man whose donkey balked until he grew so angry   15
he shoved it of a cliff. Why try to save a stubborn ass?
This too lies ahead: teaching kids to read and write,
the last career of babbling age, in a school outside of town.
When cool evening collects a larger crowd to hear you,
tell them I was born to a freedman father, and born poor,   20
but since my wings have spread out further than my nest,
what you subtract from my birth, you should add to my merits.
Say that I pleased the city's wartime and peacetime heads,
that I was short, turned gray early, like the sun's warmth,
was quick at losing my temper, quick to regain it.   25
If anyone should happen to ask you about my age,
you can say I rounded out my forty-fourth December
the year Lollius[3] brought Lepidus in as fellow consul.

---

5. This expression first appears in Terence's *Andria*
125, where Pamphilius weeps at the funeral of Chrysis.
By Horace's time it had become proverbial and usually
had an ironic flavor.
1. Horace addressed his book of epistles as if it were a
young, attractive slave eager to leave his master and
seek adventure in the larger world. First the slave "sells
himself" in the quarter of Rome where the Arcade and
a shrine of the god Vertumnus were located, shared by
booksellers and prostitutes. Then, having lost his popu-
larity, he is shipped to the provinces (a common fate for
books no longer in vogue); and his life of adventure
culminates in teaching the ABC's to children in some
provincial town (the *Epistles* become a grammar-school
textbook).
2. Ancient books were rolls of papyrus or vellum.
3. Lollius became consul in 21 B.C. The other consul-
ship had been reserved for Augustus, but when Augustus declined, Lepidus was appointed in his place.

Book II

1[1]

Since you sustain alone the many great affairs of state,
guard Italy's safety with your arms, refine our morals,
and correct our laws, I would become a public nuisance,
Caesar, if this long letter made you waste your time.
Romulus and Father Liber, Castor and Pollux, received   5
in the gods' temples when their mighty lives were done,
while yet alive and guarding mankind and the earth,
ending bloody wars, dividing fields, erecting cities,
complained that the respect they hoped for wasn't equal
to their worth. One hero[2] crushed the fearful hydra   10
and subdued other noted monsters as he did his fated tasks,
but he learned he couldn't conquer envy without dying.
For brilliance burns, and a man who weighs down others,
inferior in their gifts, won't be loved until he's gone.
To you we give full honors while you still remain,   15
placing your majesty on altars[3] for men to swear by;
we admit that none has been, nor will become, your like.
But your people, so wise and fair in this particular,
in putting you above our leaders and those the Greeks had,
don't make other judgments the same way, with similar sense;   20
for if what they're inspecting hasn't left the earth
and finished out its days they loathe and hate it.
They're so mad about antiques—the tablets of law
which the Decemvirs ordained, the royal treaties
with fair terms for both Gabinians and rugged Sabines   25
the priests' record books, the age-old prophetic scrolls—
that they insist the Muses spoke them on Mount Alba.
If just because in Greece the oldest writing is the best
we ought to use a similar scale for weighing Latin writers,
there's absolutely nothing I can say: by this logic   30
the olive can have a soft interior, the nut a soft outside,
and, having reached our peak of power, we paint and sing
and wrestle more expertly than the oiled Greeks themselves.
If aging improves poetry like wine I'd like to know
how many years it takes before a poem is any good.   35
Should a writer who passed on a hundred years ago
be counted with the old and perfect or with the new,

---

1. Horace begins this epistle to Augustus Caesar by
arguing against the overvaluation of the ancient masters
of Latin poetry and by insisting that modern poets,
himself included, not be ignored in favor of the
canonized ancients. As the epistle progresses, it en-
compasses other literary issues, such as the development of the Roman literary tradition, the spirit and role
of the writer, and Augustus' patronage of literature.
2. Hercules (see Glossary); here Horace refers to his

twelve heroic labors, which included killing and captur-
ing monsters.
3. The unofficial deification of Augustus began during
his lifetime, especially in the provinces. The only official recognition of this movement in Rome was the cult
of the Genius Augusti, which set up altars where oaths
were taken. Official and complete deification did not
occur until after Augustus' death.

and therefore bad? Draw a line, and stop all argument.
"To be old and good, a poet must lie a century in the past."
"But what if someone died a month or year too late,   40
which category for him, ancient poets or the other,
which both the present and the coming age reject?"
"Put him with the ancients; yes, he deserves a place
if he's just a month too young, or even a full year."
I'll use what you concede and from the horse's tail   45
keep plucking out the hairs, one followed by the next,
until this "dwindling heap"[4] of mine destroys my foe
who trusted in the calendar, judged quality by years,
and admired nothing that Libitina hadn't graced.
Ennius, so wise and strong, the second Homer,   50
so the critics say, seems not really to have cared
about the promise given in his Pythagorean dream.[5]
Isn't Naevius in our hands and sticking in our heads
like someone almost new? Every old poem is that sacred.
In each debate over which of them is better, we call   55
Pacuvius "old and learned," Accius "old and sublime."
We hear that Afranius' toga would have fit Menander,
that Plautus moves as easily as his model, Epicharmus,
that Caecilius succeeds with dignity, Terence with art.
These great Rome memorizes, and these she goes to see,   60
crammed inside our crowded theaters; she picks her poets
by counting heads from Livius's time until our own.
Sometimes the people sense quality, sometimes they miss.
If they so admire and praise the old poets that nothing,
they think, can be better or even as good, they're wrong.   65
If they think that much old writing is obsolete in style
and more of it is rough, if they confess it's often dull,
then they're wise, and I agree, and Jove approves.
I'm not attacking Livius's poems, not really, or urging
their destruction; after all, I learned them as a boy,   70
from Orbilius[6] the whipper. But to hear them called "correct,"
"beautiful," "just about perfect," puzzles me no end.
If perhaps one appropriate word shines out among the rest,
if one line here or there has a slightly better rhythm,
it unjustly makes the whole work go and sells it.   75
I'm offended when a poem is scorned, not for being rough,
in anyone's opinion, or sloppy, but just because it's new,
while the ancients who need excuses get honor and praise.
If I'd suggest that Atta's comedy doesn't move too well
among the saffron and the flowers, most old men would cry   80
that shame was dead; so would they if I dared to criticize
the plays in which good Aesopus and skillful Roscius starred.

---

4. The logical conundrum called *sorites*, from the Greek *soros*, "heap": "How many grains make a heap? If you take away one grain, will it remain a heap? How many grains must you remove before it no longer is a heap?" There seems to have been an analogous puzzle about how many hairs make up a tail.

5. In the *Annales* Ennius (see Glossary) related a dream in which Homer appeared and announced that Ennius himself was Homer's reincarnation, in keeping with the Pythagorean (see Glossary) doctrine of the transmigration of souls.

6. Lucius Orbilius Pupillus, teacher at the school Horace attended in Rome as a boy.

Either they'll approve only what they've liked for years,
or they hate to yield to younger men and say that works
they learned as beardless youths should be rejected now. 85
The fact is that anyone who praises Numa's Salian chant,[7]
eager to be thought an expert on what he understands no more
than I, really doesn't appreciate or like dead talent:
he's smearing *our* work, and hates and envies that and us.
Suppose the Greeks had hated novelty as much as we do? 90
What thing now would be antique? What would people have
to use as theirs, for every man to read and thumb through?
When Greece had won her wars,[8] she began to fool around,
and slid into bad conduct just when things were going well:
one moment on fire for athletes, the next for horses, 95
then mad about workers in marble, or ivory, or bronze;
she let painted canvases enchant her eyes and mind,
and sometimes loved flutists, sometimes tragic actors.
She was like a little girl playing near its nurse,
fiercely wanting, then enjoying, then forsaking. 100
That was the effect of kindly peace and favoring winds.
In Rome for ages they delighted in tradition—rising early
and keeping open house, helping clients understand the law,
lending money cautiously, to someone with an honest name,
listening to older men and explaining to those younger 105
how to increase their property, diminish harmful lust.
But what, good or bad, do you think will never change?
The capricious public has a new idea, and now it burns
with one desire: to write. Stern fathers and their sons
dine with crowns of ivy on their heads reciting verses. 110
And I, though I swear I won't compose another line,
show myself less truthful than the Parthians[9] and wake
before the sun, calling for a pen and paper and books.
Nobody ignorant of ships would sail one, and no layman
would offer wormwood to the sick: medical matters 115
are for doctors to take care of, craftsmen handle tools.
But we all, trained or not, write poems everywhere.
Yet this foolishness, this mild insanity, has virtues,
and you can judge their worth: Greed within a poet's soul
is rarely found; he loves poetry, his only passion. 120
At financial blows, fleeing slaves, and fires, he laughs;
he wouldn't think of working any fraud upon his partner
or young ward; seeds and the poorest bread sustain his life.
And though a stupid, backward soldier, he's still of social use,
if you'll allow that little things can help the great advance. 125
The poet trains the child's blurred and stammering speech,
teaches him to turn his ear away from harmful talk,
and soon with friendly words begins to shape his mind,

7. Hymns of the Salii, an ancient priesthood of Mars founded by King Numa (see Glossary); by Horace's time, the chants were unintelligible even to the priests themselves.

8. The Persian Wars in the early fifth century B.C.

were followed by an Athenian "Golden Age" of literary and artistic activity.

9. A proverbial statement, not necessarily true; after the defeat of Crassus at Carrhae the Parthians were considered the prototypical enemies of Rome.

as the corrector of fierceness and envy and wrath.
He describes fine deeds and instructs with great examples   130
each successive year; he gives the sick and hopeless comfort.
How would the chaste boys and the innocent, unwed girl
have learned the prayers without a poet given by the Muse?[1]
The chorus asks for help and feels the gods' response,
asks heaven for rain and pleases, taught how to pray;   135
it prevents disease, makes dreadful perils keep far off;
it brings us peaceful times and a season of rich crops.
The sacred song delights the gods above and those below.
Our old farmers, strong men content with what they had,
rejoiced at harvest time, refreshed body and soul too,   140
which had endured the hardship by waiting for its end.
With their fellow workers, their sons and faithful wives,
they offered Tellus a pig, milk to Silvanus, wine
and flowers to the Genius, who knows that life is short.
Fescennine verse[2] had its beginnings here, in liberty,   145
spewing barnyard insults out, one line against another;
the freedom was permitted as the years passed by,
and all enjoyed it; but then the jokes turned savage,
raged openly and entered decent homes, a menace
bound by no restrictions. Complaints were made by those   150
the bloody tooth had bitten, and even those unbitten
were concerned about the general good; so they made a law,
providing punishment, against portraying anyone in songs
that were malicious. Preferring not to die, the poets changed,
began speaking as they should and pleased the public.   155
Greece taken took her fierce captor captive[3] and bore
her arts to Latium's farms; accordingly, the crude
Saturnian measure[4] grew extinct and our old roughness
was expelled by elegance, but there long remained
and still remain today impressions of our rustic past.   160
For we didn't pay the Greeks attention until late,
didn't ask until our Punic victories[5] gave us peace
what Thespis, Sophocles, and Aeschylus could teach.
We translated them too, to see if we could do it well,
and pleased ourselves with our own nobility and force;   165
we have true tragic spirit and the gift of daring well,
but ignorantly think erasing a disgrace and fear it.
It's thought, since comic subjects come from daily life,
that writing comedy costs little sweat; no, comedy is worse,
because it's an easier thing to judge. Consider Plautus,   170

1. Refers to Horace's own *Carmen Saeculare*, composed for the great Roman festival of 17 B.C.; it was sung by a chorus of young boys and girls. Horace proceeds, in 134–138, to delineate the function of the chorus, especially in connection with hymns offered during religious ceremonies.

2. The earliest Italian drama; vestiges of it appeared in the bawdy songs of abuse sung at triumphs and weddings.

3. Although Rome had conquered and now controlled Greece, the older country's art and literature exercised a powerful sway over the tastes and aspirations of the Roman intelligentsia.

4. The ancient Italian meter seen in many inscriptions and used by Naevius in his epic *Bellum Poenicum*; dactylic hexameter, adapted from Greek epic, soon replaced it.

5. Rome gradually superseded Carthage (founded by Phoenicians, *Poeni*) as the dominant power in the western Mediterranean in a series of three Punic Wars (264–241 B.C.; 218–201 B.C.; 149–146 B.C.).

his characters—the typical young man in love,
the stingy father, the clever, treacherous pimp,
his greedy parasites all modeled on Dossennus[6]—
and how he runs across the stage in floppy socks.[7]
Platus wants money to put into his box, after that   175
he doesn't care if his play falls or keeps its feet.
And those Fame's windblown car has carried to the stage
are deflated by a sluggish viewer, inflated by a live one.
So trifling, so petty a thing can destroy or save a soul
that thirsts for praise. Goodbye to comedy, I say,   180
if praise denied makes me a skeleton, granted makes me fat.
Often even a brave poet will be terrified and run,
for the many have the smaller share of worth and honor;
they're illiterate and dense, and glad to slug the knight
who crosses them. In the middle of a play they'll shout   185
for boxers or a bear, the kind of thing the mob enjoys.
And now, even from the ears of knights all pleasure's gone,
to follow after restless, wavering eyes and empty shows.
The stage remains four hours and more without a curtain
while squads of horsemen, companies of foot go dashing by. 190
Soon unhappy kings are dragged along in captive's bonds,
then chariots, carriages, wagons, ships charge past,
and captured ivory is borne across, and captured Corinth.[8]
If he were still on earth, Democritus[9] would laugh
whether a hybrid monstrosity, a camelopard,   195
or a white elephant made the gaping people stare;
he'd look at them with full attention, not the stage,
as a far more monstrous and entertaining sight.
Also, he'd think our authors wrote plays for asses
who were deaf, for what voice is powerful enough   200
to overcome the sounds that fill our theaters?
You'd swear that a storm was ripping Mount Garganus
or the Tuscan Sea, so much noise goes with the show
and greets the foreign jewelry which coats the actors
to make the audience applaud them on the stage.   205
"What did he say?" "Nothing." "What makes them clap?"
"His robe's stained poison purple with Tarentine dye."
By the way, if you think that I, who won't write plays,
don't properly appreciate what others do so well,
any poet seems to me to be dancing on a wire   210
who affects my soul with what really isn't there,
disturbs it, calms it down, fills it with false terrors,
and magically drops me now in Thebes and now in Athens.
But also think of those who prefer a reader as a judge
instead of a proud viewer whose scorn they'd have to bear, 215
and notice them a little if you want to see your gift,[1]

6. A character of the popular native Atellan farce; Plautus' parasites resembled him more closely than the parasites of Greek New Comedy.

7. He was a careless writer. The *soccus* or sock was a slipper worn by comic actors; the *cothurnus* or buskin, a boot worn in tragedy. Each type of footwear came to symbolize the type of drama in which it was worn.

8. Spoils of bronze from Corinth, a city proverbial for its fine work in that metal.

9. Traditionally called the "laughing philosopher," since he was in the habit of laughing at human folly instead of excoriating it.

1. The Palatine Library, which Augustus has established for public use. See *E*.I.3.17 and note.

so worthy of Apollo, well stocked with books, and to spur
your singers toward green Helicon more warmly than before.
Of course, we poets often get ourselves in trouble
(I slash my vines) when we present you with our books   220
although you're tired or engaged; when we're insulted
because a friend has dared to criticize a single line;
when, unencored, we turn back to sections just recited;
when we complain that our hard work and the texture
of our poems, so nicely spun, aren't well appreciated;   225
when we hope so far as this: that once you know
that we're composing, you'll kindly, voluntarily
call us in, forbid our poverty, and order us to write.
But, even so, you would do well to analyze our work,
for we guard the temples where your merit will reside.   230
In war and peace it shines; don't trust it to bad poets.
King Alexander the Great was charmed by Choerilus,
who, for his unrefined, abortive verse, in his ledger
noted down a sum of royal money, golden Philips.[2]
But just as ink will leave a mark on what it touches,   235
a dirty stain, so often writers with their ugly songs
smear shining deeds. That spendthrift king who paid
so high a price for such a silly poem forbade by law
that anyone except Apelles should ever paint
or any sculptor but Lysippus mold in bronze   240
the face of mighty Alexander. But if you observed
his judgment, so exacting in the visual arts,
in books and what the Muses have to give,
you'd swear that he was born among Boeotia's fogs.[3]
Your judgment, however, and the patronage you give,   245
bringing credit both to you and those you've helped,
aren't shamed by Varius and Vergil, your beloved poets.
Nor are faces better captured on bronze statues
than in poets' work are shown the nature and the spirit
of great men. And I, rather than these conversations,[4]   250
which creep along the ground, would write an epic
and picture the entire earth, the rivers, the forts
high-perched among the rocks, the barbarous kingdoms—
a world which, thanks to you, has ended all its wars.
I would picture Janus[5] with closed gates guarding peace,   255
and the Rome the Parthians fear, with you our leader,
if what I wanted to do, I could do. But your grandeur
won't accept a little poem, nor will my modesty dare
to start a task my powers would decline to carry through.
Besides, it's stupid to pester anyone you care about,   260
and the vilest way to do it is with meter and with "art."
For we all more quickly learn and easily remember

2. Coins stamped with the image of Philip of Macedon,
Alexander's father.
3. The lowland climate of this Greek region supposedly
caused its inhabitants to become dull-witted.
4. Meaning his own *Satires* and *Epistles*, which he
calls *sermones*, ''conversations.''

5. The doors to the temple of Janus were traditionally
closed during peacetime and opened when war was
declared.

the poems we scorn than those we approve of and respect.
I don't like graceless honors for myself, a wax bust
set up somewhere that makes me uglier than I am,   265
or a sloppy, awkward poem in which I'm glorified.
That idiotic gift would make me blush and insure
my passage in a box, a kind of coffin, with my poet,
to the market where people sell incense and perfume
and pepper, and anything wrapped up in wasted paper.   270

2

Dear Florus, noble, good Tiberius's faithful friend,
suppose a dealer offered you a slave, a native
of Tibur or of Gabii, and made this pitch: "The boy
is light-complexioned, a fine specimen from head to toe,
and he's yours, now and forever, for 8,000 sesterces.   5
A house-bred slave, he's very eager; nod and he jumps.
He knows a smattering of Greek and can pick up any skill,
just name it: the boy's wet clay, mold him yourself.
He even sings; no training, but he's fine over a drink.
Big promises won't build your confidence; when men praise   10
too heavily what they sell, they're trying to get rid of it.
But not me, I don't have to; I'm poor, but I don't owe.
No one in the business makes deals like this; I wouldn't,
except to you. Oh, he got lazy once and hid (they all do)
beneath the stairs, frightened of the whip upon the wall."   15
If, after hearing that, you took the deal, the dealer
could take your money and not be penalized; I'd judge
you bought flawed goods knowingly and were legally informed.
Would you then chase him and involve him in a case you'd lose?
I said when you left that I was lazy, almost (I said)   20
a cripple at this work, to keep you from getting sore
and scolding when your letters to me didn't get replies.
But what's the good of being protected by the law
if you still object? On top of that, you even claim
I haven't sent some promised poems, that I'm a liar.   25
A soldier of Lucullus saved his wages through a campaign
that was hard, but one night, worn out and snoring,
was relieved of every cent. Then, as angry at himself
as at the foe, he raged like a fierce and hungry wolf.
The story says he drove the royal troops opposing him   30
from a site well fortified and full of treasure.
The deed made him famous; he was gloriously decorated
and received a bonus too, 20,000 sesterces in cash.
A little later his chief needed some stronghold taken,
I don't know which, and tried to stir the soldier up   35
with words that would have given even cowards heart.
"Go, good man, where honor calls you; go, and good luck.
Your merit will win you great reward. Well, why don't you go?"
The man was a peasant, but no fool. "Someone else will go,"
he said, "go where you like; just be sure he's lost his money."   40

I was raised in Rome where my fate brought me, and there
I learned how much Achilles' anger[1] hurt the Greeks.
Then moral Athens gave me some finesse, a little bit,
which made me want to tell the crooked from the straight
and within the Academic groves go seeking after truth.   45
But the fierce age thrust me from that happy place,
and the fever of the state drove war's tyro into arms
that for Augustus Caesar's strength were no fair match.
As soon as Philippi had dismissed me from the front,
humbled with clipped wings, all my father left me lost,   50
both house and farm, audacious poverty forced me
to write verses.[2] But now, lacking nothing that I need,
what quantity of hemlock[3] would ever be enough to cure me,
if I didn't think it a better thing to sleep than write?
The passing years rob us of our pleasures one by one.   55
They've taken jokes and sex away, and games and dinners;
now they're clutching at my poems. How can I fight that?
Besides, not everyone likes and admires the same stuff.
Lyric pleases you, another man delights in iambs,
still another in Bion's satire[4] and coarse black salt.   60
Any three guests I have seem almost never to agree;
their tastes differ and they ask for different things.
What should I serve? What not serve? You reject their choices,
the other two think yours is bitter, really revolting.
And finally, how can you believe that Rome's a place   65
where I can write, with so much happening, so many chores?
This man wants a sponsor, that an audience—as if I
were totally free; one sick friend lies on the Quirinal Hill,
another past the Aventine, and I've got to visit both.
That's a nice, convenient distance, isn't it? "Well,   70
the streets are empty, nothing stops you from composing."
Just a builder with mules and porters in a furious rush,
a giant crane lifting now a beam and now a boulder,
howling funeral trains tangled up with heavy wagons,
a mad dog running here, and there a speedy, slimy sow.   75
You try it, take a walk and make up pretty verses!
The whole poetic chorus loves the groves and flees the city,
good followers of Bacchus, who delights in sleep and shade.
But you expect me, with all this racket night and day,
to go on singing and to travel in the poet's narrow road.   80

---

1. See *E*.1.2.12 and note.
2. Horace's father brought him to Rome from provincial Venusia so that he could obtain a quality education; as a youth, Horace went to Athens to continue his studies (the normal "higher education" for a young Roman man of breeding). While Horace was still in Athens, the assassination of Julius Caesar in 44 B.C. split the Roman world into two factions. When Brutus visited Athens on his way to Asia Minor in the summer of 44, Horace, about twenty-one at the time, joined his staff as a military tribune. The Battle of Philippi in 42 brought the defeat of Brutus; Horace left the Republican faction and returned to Rome to find that his property had been confiscated. He then took a job as clerk in the treasury department and, shortly thereafter, began to make a name for himself as a writer.
3. The purgative effect of small doses of hemlock was believed to cure madness.
4. Bion, an Athenian philosopher of the early third century B.C., studied in the Academy. In addition, he was strongly influenced by Crates the Cynic and Theodorus the atheistic hedonist; nevertheless, his writings, which influenced later Roman satire, employed an extremely eclectic style which paid homage to no one philosophical school. "Coarse black salt" refers to Bion's cynical, caustic humor.

A scholar who chose calm Athens as a place to live
spent seven years in study; among books and theories
he grew old, he became more silent than a statue,
and all who saw him laughed so hard they shook. Can I,
here, swamped by so many things, deluged by this city,   85
ask myself to link together words that fit the lyre?
Two lawyer brothers lived in Rome; one read and one pled,
and each regularly gave the other undiluted praise.
One became a Gracchus; the other, a Mucius in return.
Why should this insanity plague warbling poets any less?   90
I write lyrics, he writes elegies. "A gorgeous vision!
your poem, adorned by all nine Muses!" Now, notice
how proudly, how very importantly we gaze around us
in this shrine[5] that accepts Rome's poets on its shelves.
And if you have the time, come close and hear the praise   95
each brings the other, from which we weave our crowns.
I get a good beating, and I clobber my opponent
as we slow Samnites[6] duel until the first lamp's lit.
His ballot makes me Alcaeus; and mine makes him?
Whom but Callimachus? If he seems to want still more,   100
let him be Mimnermus, any name he chooses that inflates.
It's hard to please the poets, that irritable race,
as I must while writing and trying to get votes.
But if I abandon all ambition and repossess my soul
I can cover up my ears at readings and not be punished.   105
Composers of bad poems are laughed at; however,
they love writing and admire themselves and will, gladly,
if you say nothing, praise whatever they've composed.
But anyone who wants to write an authentic poem
needs an honest censor's soul as much as paper.   110
He must be firm: words which lack sufficient dignity
or don't make clear sense should not be circulated;
so he'll throw them out, even those that hate to go
and have spent their time in Vesta's temple[7] until now.
What the people buried long ago, the good poet unearths,   115
restoring to the light the splendid names for things
once spoken by old Cato and Cethegus, but at present
abandoned in their age, made to look odd by neglect.
He enlists new words which modern usage has brought forth.
Clear and strong, flowing smoothly in an unchoked stream,   120
the poet pours his wealth on Latium, a treasure of words.
He cuts back wild growths, carefully smooths passages
which seem too rough, takes out whatever has no strength.
He seems to play, but really he works, like a dancer
who's first a satyr on the stage, then rustic Cyclops.   125
I wouldn't mind being called lazy and sloppy

5. The temple of Apollo on the Palatine housed the famous public library of Rome.
6. Gladiators wearing heavy armor, which enabled them to fight for a long time without sustaining serious injury.

7. Vesta was goddess of the hearth and household. Her temple at the east end of the Forum, tended by Vestal Virgins, was emblematic of Rome's most cherished institutions.

if my bad work seemed good to me, or at least not bad:
better than knowing and suffering. A wealthy Argive[8]
once imagined he was watching tragic actors of great skill
inside an empty theater where he happily sat and clapped.   130
The usual tasks of life he carried out quite well;
he was a considerate neighbor, a gracious host,
an obliging husband, a master who forgave his slaves
when they broke a bottle's seal, instead of having fits,
and he always kept away from cliffs and open wells.   135
Then his family, which cared and helped, arranged a cure.
Straight hellebore[9] cleaned out his bile and his mind,
and he became himself again. "Ah, you've killed me, friends,
not saved me," he said. "You took away my pleasure,
expelled by force the little lapse that gave me joy."   140
But surely it's right to finish trifling, to grow wise
and concede to boys the sports proper for youth's season;
to look no more for words that fit the Latin lyre,
but learn instead the notes and rhythms of real life.[1]
And so I turn certain questions over in my mind.   145
If no quantity of water is enough to quench your thirst,
you tell the doctor; if the more money that you gain
the more you want, do you dare not confess that illness?
If you have a wound which the herbs and roots prescribed
don't help to heal, you'll throw away the roots and herbs   150
which don't contribute to your cure. You may have heard
that men to whom the gods give riches are freed from evil
foolishness, but since you're not one bit smarter,
although richer, how can you accept that old advice?
But if wealth had the virtue of making you more wise,   155
less grasping, less of a coward, surely you would blush
if one man lived upon the earth more stingily than you.
Ownership can be secured with copper and with scales,[2]
and also, if you believe the laws, by right of use.
Yours is the farm that feeds you, and Orbius' steward,[3]   160
harrowing the soil which soon will grow your grain,
makes you his boss. You pay the money and take the grapes,
chickens, eggs, jug of wine; in doing this, you see,
you buy a little at a time a farm that may have cost
three hundred thousand, maybe even more, when sold.   165
What's the difference when you pay, now or in the past?
The buyer, years ago, of a farm near Veii or Aricia
always buys the greens he eats, though he thinks not,
buys on chilly evenings the wood which fires his stove.
But he calls all his before the poplar on the line   170
that keeps him out of battles with the neighbors, as if

8. A native of Argos, in Greece.
9. See *S.*II.3.82 and note.
1. Horace reiterates his decision to give up lyric poetry
in favor of philosophy and the pursuit of moral wisdom.
2. Traditional symbols associated with the purchase of
property.

3. Horace argues that, although the landowner Orbius
is the steward's master, the man who really benefits
from the steward's labor is the man who eats the grain.

something could be owned which in an hour's swift space
may by gift or sale or violence, or by all-composing death,
change masters and fall beneath another man's control.
So since to none perpetual use is given, and one heir   175
succeeds the next as wave rolls down upon the wave before,
what are estates or granaries worth? Why to Calabrian
fields add new land in Lucania, if Orcus harvests
great and small together and gold can't buy him off?
Jewels, marble, ivory, Etruscan statues, paintings,   180
silver, clothing tinted purple with Gaetulian dye—
most don't have these things; one man doesn't want them.
Why one brother prefers unguents, idleness, and fun
to owning Herod's profitable palms[4] while the other,
rich and energetic, from sunrise to evening shade   185
tames forests with fire, farmland with the iron plow,
the Genius knows, the partner who controls our natal star
and, as human nature's mortal god, shows every man
a different face, varying from glad to gloomy.
I'll use my modest wealth, take from it what I need   190
and never worry about my heir's opinion of me
when he sees how small his share is. But I also
want to learn how much a liberal, generous man
is different from a spendthrift, and a saver from a miser.
They do differ: you can waste money like a prodigal   195
or you can spend without pain and not earn too much,
be like the boy you were at spring vacation long ago
delighting in your brief and happy time while it remains.
May black poverty stay distant from my home, and whether
I ride in a small ship or a big, may I always be myself.   200
I'm not driven with puffed sails by the strong north wind
or beaten by the southern gales because I go against them;
in gifts, appearance, goodness, status, wisdom, wealth,
I'm last among the leaders, always first of those who trail.
You're not stingy; good. But, along with avarice, did all   205
other vices flee? Is false ambition absent from your soul?
Fear of death, and anger at death—are they absent too?
Dreams, magic's terrors, prodigies, fortune tellers,
night spirits, Thessalian hexes—do you laugh at these?
Do you count birthdays gladly? Do you forgive your friends?   210
Have you become milder and better as old age draws close?
What relief can you gain by removing one thorn of many?
If you don't know how to live right, yield to those who do.
You've played enough, have done enough eating and boozing;
the time to leave is now; for if you take too many drinks,   215
young men, with a right to revel, will laugh and push you out.

---

4. The dates from the palm groves around Jericho were an excellent source of profit for Herod the Great, King of Judaea in 39–34 B.C.

3
Ars Poetica[1]

Suppose a painter chose to place a human head
upon a horse's neck, to lay feathers of all colors
on organs gathered from all over, to make his figure
a black, disgusting fish below, on top a lovely girl.
Given a private view, my friends, how couldn't you laugh?   5
Believe me, Pisos, this painting and a kind of poem
are very similar, one like an image in a sick man's dream,
a fever image whose head and foot can't possibly belong
upon the same physique. "The painters and the poets both
have always shared the right of doing what they like."   10
Yes, we seek this indulgence and we grant it in return,
but not to couple fierce and gentle creatures, not to
pair together snakes and birds or lambs and tigers.
Quite often works heroically begun and very promising
have here and there a widely gleaming purple patch   15
stitched to them, so that Diana's grove and altar,
the quick stream flowing through the pleasant fields,
the Rhine and rainbow are all described at length.
But they shouldn't be, not out of place. Perhaps a cypress
is your specialty, but what if you've been hired to paint   20
a hopeless swimmer, after a shipwreck? An amphora began
to grow—why does the whirling wheel bring forth a jug?
In short, make an unbroken unity of every work you try.
Most poets, father and young men deserving such a father,
go wrong in trying to be right: I struggle for concision,   25
I wind up being obscure; others try for smoothness
and lose strength, or for sublimity, and get gas.
One poet, too cautious, fears storms and crawls along,
the other craves bizarre variety in a single subject
and paints a dolphin in a forest, a boar among the waves.   30
Fear of criticism leads to faults if we lack art.
Near the Aemilian School[2] a sculptor lives, a clever man
at shaping fingernails and catching flowing hair in bronze,
but the total effect is weak; he can't create a whole,
he doesn't know how. If I cared about good composition,   35
I'd no more copy him than like living with a crooked nose
even if dark eyes and hair still made me worth a look.
Writers, choose a subject for which your talent is a match
and take your time considering what your shoulders can't

1. *The Ars Poetica* is a basic document in criticism, a source for many traditional ideas about literature. For such an important work, it is remarkably controversial. Scholars have argued about its date of composition, its proper title, and the identity of the Pisos, its recipients. They are also in disagreement over weightier matters, such as the meaning of certain passages and lines (some of them very important in the history of criticism), the structure of the poem, or even whether or not it has a structure, and the question of its quality as criticism and as poetry. Readers should perhaps be reminded that the *Ars* is an epistle—a letter—and not a formal treatise.
2. A gladiatorial school.

and can endure; a man who picks what suits his powers   40
won't find himself deserted by eloquence or by clear order.
Order has a special quality and charm, in my opinion:
the poet says right now exactly what he must say now
and postpones other things which for the moment he ignores.
Do as much in every line; be both careful and precise   45
with any promised poem, choosing this word, spurning that.
You've written very well if, by placing it with skill,
you make a known word new. If, by chance, it's necessary
to shed light on something recent requiring new expressions,
you can fashion words the belted Cethegi[3] never heard.   50
We shouldn't overuse this license, but we have it.
Words newly made are well received if flowing
from Greek sources in a narrow stream. But why
does Rome grant Plautus and Caecilius what it won't
to Vergil and to Varius? Why am I offending if I add   55
the few I have? Didn't the speech of Ennius and Cato
enrich the language of our land and invent new names
to give to things? It has been and always will be right
that words are coined which bear the imprint of the present.
As forests change their leaves with every passing year,   60
the old ones falling down, so, as older words die out,
the newborn, like all children, grow and strengthen.
Death has a claim on us and all we have. Now Neptune
is received on land to guard our ships from northern winds,
a regal work; a swamp, long sterile, which only oars   65
could cross, feeds nearby towns and feels the heavy plow;
a river inhospitable to crops is taught a better route
and flows along it. But all that mortals make will die,
and language has yet a briefer span of pleasing, lovely life.
Many words now fallen will be reborn and others fall   70
that now hold worthy places; use determines this,
it controls the judging, law, and standard of our speech.
Exploits of kings and warrior chiefs, disastrous wars—
Homer made clear the meter one should use for these.[4]
The couplet with unequal lines first enclosed laments,   75
and then was used in giving thanks for granted prayers;
but just what poet first composed the little elegy
scholars keep disputing, and the case remains in court.
Archilochus' furious rage armed him with the iamb,
the meter both the sock and buskin took as theirs;   80
it was perfect for trading speeches and overcoming
the noises of the crowd, and with action it went well.
The subjects given by the Muse for singing on the lyre
were the gods and their children, the victories of boxers
and of steeds, young love affairs, and carefree drinking.   85
Since the poetic forms and styles are definitely set,

3. Men of the old Republic, such as the famous orator
Cethegus, had worn the *cinctus* (a sort of loincloth)
instead of the tunic as an undergarment.
4. Dactylic hexameter, the meter of the *Iliad* and *Odys-*

sey. Horace proceeds (through 82) to state the meters
appropriate to other genres: the couplet, made up of a
hexameter and a pentameter, for elegy; and the iambic
trimeter for dramatic dialogue.

why call me a poet if I don't know how to follow them?
Why am I ignorant through false pride when I could learn?
Tragic lines don't give comic themes a setting they enjoy;
equally resented is comic speech, words almost proper   90
for the sock, when used to sing about Thyestes' feast.[5]
Each literary kind should keep its rightful place.
Yet occasions come when comedy will raise its voice
and raging Chremes swell his mouth and fiercely scold;
at times a tragic figure will lament in common speech   95
(as do Telephus and Peleus, both poor and in exile,
abandoning their bombast and sesquipedalian words),
if he wants his misery to touch his audience's heart.
It isn't enough to make lines pretty; they must move,
and affect the hearer's soul exactly as the poet wants.   100
Just as laughter inspires laughter, tears bring tears
to human faces; if you want my tears, you first must
weep yourself. Then your agonies will hurt me too,
Telephus or Peleus. But if your lines don't fit you,
I may sleep, or I may laugh. Sad words go with gloom   105
upon a face, words full of threats fit angry looks.
Light chatter suits a smile, serious talk a frown.
For nature moves us inwardly in response to every guise
that fortune wears; it brings us pleasure, fuels our wrath,
crushes us to earth beneath our sorrow, tortures us,   110
and then, with speech, brings out the motions of the soul.
If a character's words aren't proper for his place,
Roman knights and infantry alike will loudly boo.
A hero and a god should speak quite differently,
so should a vigorous old man and a fiery youth   115
in bloom, a matron of high station and a busy nurse,
a roving merchant and the tiller of a thriving field,
a Colchian and an Assyrian, an Argive and a Theban.
Either be traditional or make the characters consistent.
Writer, if you've chosen to show great Achilles[6] once again,   120
active, angry, inexorable, have him fiercely deny
law's hold on him and claim by violence what he likes.
Let Medea be savage and relentless, Ino full of tears,
Ixion treacherous, Io far-wandering, Orestes sad.
But if, in trying something new on stage, you dare   125
invent a character, keep him to the very end
as he was at his first entrance, entirely consistent.
It's hard to express the universal in your own way,
and you'll do better spinning Troy's story into plays
than being first to stage events unvoiced and overlooked.   130
Public subjects[7] will become your private property, if
you neither plod along the common, easy, circling path

---

5. In myth, Thyestes seduced Aerope, the wife of his brother Atreus. In revenge Atreus invited Thyestes to a banquet and served Thyestes the flesh of his own children as food. The story was the subject for many tragedies.

6. See *E*.I.2.12 and note.
7. Material provided by Homer and by myth and legend in general.

nor strain to match your model word for word, too close
in your translation; for imitating will put you in a trap
where you'll be kept, either by your pride or by generic law.   135
Don't begin like this, as the cyclic poets[8] used to:
"Of Priam's destiny I'll sing, and of the war renowned."
What can this big-mouthed boaster bring to equal that?
The mountains heave and give birth to a tiny mouse.
Another poet[9] does much better without the clumsy start.   140
"Tell me, Muse, about the man who, when Troy had fallen,
saw the cities and the ways of life of many peoples."
To give, not smoke from roaring flame, but light from smoke
is his intention, and so he offers us amazing creatures,
Antiphates and Scylla, the Cyclops and Charybdis.   145
He doesn't begin Diomedes' return with Meleager's death[1]
or the Trojan War with the egg that hatched the twins.
Always he goes right to the point, midway in the action,
as if all his readers knew what went before; he grips us,
and if he can't make something shine, he cuts it out.   150
He lies in such a way, making truth and fiction blend,
that beginning and middle, middle and end won't disagree.
Poet, hear what I, and the people too, require
if you want to keep us in our seats until the curtain,
all set to clap when the singer tells us, "Now applaud."   155
Correctly represent the marks of every phase of life,
and give your characters what suits their varying years.
A little boy, a recent talker who firmly plants his feet
upon the ground, loves playing with his friends, flies
in and out of rages for no reason, and changes every hour.   160
A young man, still beardless, but finally on his own,
loves dogs and horses and the sunny, grassy field.
He's wax for vice to shape, thorny to good advice,
slow to acquire things he needs, careless with cash,
proud and demanding, quick to drop what he once loved.   165
An adult has concerns that fit his grown-up mind;
a slave to his position, he seeks power and connections,
avoids commitments that later may be difficult to change.
An old man's life is full of irritation, for either
he's greedy and miserable, afraid to use his savings,   170
or he worries and delays no matter what he does.
He stalls, keeps hoping, does nothing, wants to stay alive,
grouches and complains; he's a praiser of the vanished past
when he was young, censurer and critic of those young now.
Much that we enjoy comes with the years as they advance.   175
Much, as they recede, goes with them. Rather than give
old men's lines to young men or adult roles to boys,

---

8. Epic poets inferior to Homer. Their work added to
his formed a complete "cycle" of poems about Troy.
9. Homer. Lines 141–42 paraphrase the opening lines
of the *Odyssey*.
1. Meleager was the uncle of Diomedes and thus belonged to the generation before him. In the following
line, the "egg that hatched the twins" refers to the birth

of Castor, Pollux, Helen, and Clytemnestra from the
union of Leda and the swan. Thus Homer does not begin
the story of Diomedes' return from Troy with the tragic
death of his uncle many years before, nor does he begin
the story of the Trojan War with the birth of Helen, who
caused it.

always be sure that every age receives its proper traits.
Action either happens on the stage or is reported there.
Anything we learn of through the ear less moves the mind 180
than something shown our trusted eyes, offered firsthand
to the spectator. But if a scene belongs offstage,
don't push it on; many things aren't suitable for eyes
which an actor soon appearing can vividly describe.
For Medea shouldn't kill her sons before the audience 185
or evil Atreus cook human guts in public view,
or Procne be transformed to a bird, Cadmus to a snake.
Anything like that you show me I'll disbelieve and hate.
Neither drop below nor raise past five the acts presented
in a play if you want it to be called for and shown again. 190
Let no god meddle without a knot that no one but a god
could loose, and don't let fourth characters butt in.
The chorus should work like an actor, with a real role,
and not step out of it by singing intermission songs
which don't help the play go forward and fit in well. 195
It should support the good and offer friendly counsel,
calm down furious men, cherish those who dislike vice;
it should praise plain living, praise healthful justice
and law, as well as the peace that comes with open doors.
Have it keep confidences safe and ask the gods in prayers 200
that favor be returned to humble men and leave the proud.
The pipe, not the modern, brass-ringed version, rival
to the horn, but with few holes and thin and simple,
once aided and accompanied the chorus by itself, and
its music filled the theater, then not too crowded. 205
The people gathered there in numbers you could count,
and they were decent and modest in their tastes.
But after becoming conquerors, gaining new land, enlarging
their growing city's walls, they drank at festivals by day
to celebrate the Genius of each man and went unpunished. 210
Then greater liberty was given to rhythm and to meter.
What did they know? A mixed bag of holidaying rubes
and city people, of aristocrats and common clods.
So to the ancient art the piper added luxury and dance
and trailed his flowing robes as he swept across the stage; 215
so the lyre, once such a simple thing, increased its notes,
and rhetoric without restraint produced a novel style
while profound remarks and prophecies were uttered
that in meaning were no clearer than the oracles of Delphi.[2]
A competitor in tragic song who sought to win the goat[3] 220
soon took away the forest satyrs' clothes[4] (though crude,
he kept his dignity through all the fooling) because

2. Traditionally couched in obscure language.
3. It was commonly believed that the word "tragedy" originally meant "goat-song," since the victor in the dramatic contest was supposedly awarded a goat *(tragos)*.
4. The satyr-play was closely connected with tragedy; though not comedy, it was more burlesque in its treat-

ment of mythological themes than tragedy. It was presented as the fourth play after each tragic trilogy at the Greek drama festivals. There is no evidence that Roman satyr-plays were ever performed. Horace may be thinking of Roman plays resembling them, such as the Atellan farces, or he may have been interested in establishing them on the Roman stage.

that was the bait and pleasing freshness which could hold
a viewer with his sacrifices made, drunk and feeling wild.
But be careful how you represent your laughing jokers,   225
the satyrs, and how you move from serious to funny.
Don't let any god that you might show, or any hero
who just appeared dressed royally in gold and purple,
sound as if he always spent his time in crummy bars,
or, if he avoids the dirt, reach out for clouds and air.   230
Spouting funny lines is below the place of tragedy.
She's like a fine lady at a festival who has to dance,
and nothing like the satyrs; she's bashful, they're loud.
I wouldn't reject all words but the very simplest
and plainest, if, Pisos, I ever wrote a satyr play,   235
or try so hard to make my style consistently untragic
that Davus[5] wouldn't differ when he speaks from reckless
Pythias, who pulled Simo's nose and took his money,
or from Silenus, tutor and servant to a youthful god.
I'd make my poem of known materials, so that anyone   240
might hope to match me, but he'd work and sweat in vain
if he dared try: that's the power of order and arrangement,
that is the effect of style when working with the ordinary.
Fauns brought from the forest to the stage, in my opinion,
shouldn't turn into natives of the streets, almost the Forum,   245
either by behaving like young studs in love and crooning
or by firing out a fusillade of disgusting dirty jokes.
That's how you anger men with horses, fathers, and money,
and though the pea and nut gallery might enjoy the play,
the others won't sit still for it, let alone crown it.   250
Long syllable following short is called an iamb,[6]
a quick foot; so the iambic line (as the iamb asked)
was called a "trimeter" although it held six beats
arranged the same from start to finish. But recently,
to reach the ear more slowly with slightly greater force,   255
it became a father to adopted sons, slow spondees,
and was considerate and kind, though more than equal,
for it kept the second and fourth feet. But Accius
in his famed trimeters used the iamb rarely, and Ennius
delivered to the stage lines burdened by enormous weight.   260
Either he was too hasty a worker, and too imprecise,
or he had no sense of art; his few iambs accuse him.
Not all critics recognize bad meter when they see it,
and pardons are given undeserved to Roman poets.
So, should I scrawl and ramble as I like? Or assume   265
that everyone will spot my errors and play it safe,
pardonable and cautious? I'd dodge attacks by doing that,
but I wouldn't merit praise. Make your models Greek,
and turn their pages nightly; turn them daily too.

5. Davus, Pythias, and Simo were standard names, respectively, for the slave, the prostitute, and the old man of comedy. Silenus, the old guardian and attendant of Dionysus, was a common figure of the satyr-play.

6. Iambic trimeter was the standard meter for dramatic dialogue. See 79–82.

I know your ancestors praised Plautus, for his meter   270
and his jokes; they were too charitable on either count
(I won't say stupid). Well, they liked him. But you and I,
we understand how a coarse line differs from a clever one,
and our ears or fingers tell us if the meter is correct.
The invention of the tragic genre, unknown till then,   275
is credited to Thespis, who used wagons for his stages
where players sang and acted, their faces smeared with lees.
After him came the creator of the tragic mask and robe,
Aeschylus, also first to raise the stage a bit on beams
and to teach actors to project and wear high buskins.   280
Next Old Comedy arrived and gained no small amount
of praise; but its freedom slid to vice, to violence
needing law's restraint. Law was imposed, the chorus
silenced and ashamed, and it lost its right to wound.
Not a single opportunity did our poets leave untried,   285
nor were they least successful when they dared to step
from Greece's path and sing about Italian themes
in tragedies and comedies attired in Roman clothes.[7]
No stronger in our courage or in our glorious arms
would Latium be than in our language, except that every   290
single poet hates slow going and working with a file.
Sons of Pompilius,[8] reject any poem which much time
and much erasing haven't carefully refined, and which
they haven't smoothed ten times to meet the testing nail.
Since genius seems a pleasanter thing than painful art,   295
as Democritus believed (who then excluded all sane bards
from Helicon), most men who write trim neither nails
nor beards; they seek out hiding places, shun the baths.
For anyone can win a poet's name and with it the rewards
if he never brings his head, too mad for Anticyra[9] tripled,   300
to Licinus the barber. What makes me such a fool?
I purge myself of bile at the start of every spring.
No poet could outwrite me if I didn't. But since
nothing's worth that, I'll be a whetstone and restore
the edge to others' blades, do no cutting for myself.   305
I won't write, but I'll teach the writer's trade and duties:
where to get material, what feeds and forms a poet,
what is right, what isn't, where truth and error lead.
Good writing has its source, its origin, in good thinking.
Your subject you can find revealed in Socrates' pages;   310
your words will follow the subject without being forced.
A poet must learn what is owed to country and to friends,
how a parent is loved, and a brother, and a guest,
what the duties are of senator and judge, what tasks
a general has when sent to war; with all this understood,   315

---

7. Comedies and tragedies with native Italian themes, called *fabulae togatae* and *fabulae praetextae*. It is probable that in comedy the actors wore the Roman toga; in serious plays they wore the *praetexta*, the dress of a Roman magistrate.

8. The Pisos claimed descent from Calpus, one of the sons of King Numa Pompilius.
9. See *S*.II.3.82 and note.

the poet is equipped to make each character authentic.
I'll order this learned imitator to take life, real manners,
for his model, and draw living voices from that source.
Sometimes a few good speeches that fit the speakers
make a graceless play without fine language or much style,   320
have stronger appeal and more interest for the people
than one with pointless verses and tuneful little frills.
Greek genius and Greek mastery of words were given
by the Muse to a nation greedy just for fame.
Roman boys have calculation drill based on the penny   325
and learn to divide it by a hundred. "Next question,
Albinus Jr. If from five-twelfths, you take away one,
what's left? Come on, you know it." "A third?" "Great!
You're in business! Now add a twelfth instead. What then?"
"One-half." But this concern with money rusts our souls   330
and once they're ruined, what poems can we expect to write
worth coating with protective oils and storing in fine wood?
Poets intend to give either pleasure or instruction
or to combine the pleasing and instructive in one poem.
Be concise in all you teach, so that attentive minds   335
can quickly see your point and remember it correctly;
everything poured into a full memory will flow back out.
Inventions made for pleasure must seem quite probable:
your story shouldn't ask belief for anything it likes,
and extract a living boy from Lamia's belly after lunch.   340
The ranks of older men sneer at poems without a message,
haughtily young knights reject the poems they find austere.
The poet winning every vote blends the useful with the sweet,
giving pleasure to his reader while he offers him advice.
His book will make the Sosii money and travel overseas,   345
and far into the years ahead extend its author's name.
There are some errors that we're willing to ignore:
a tone the ear and mind desire can falter on the string,
and when seeking a low note we so often get a shrill.
No bow aimed at a target can hit it every time.   350
So when most of a poem shines brilliantly, I'm not bothered
by its spots, the few that inattention chanced to spill
or human weakness didn't see. But here's my point:
A scribe who makes the same mistake throughout his copy,
though often warned, receives no pardon, and a singer   355
raises laughter at himself by always missing the same note.
Any poet who keeps slipping up is a Choerilus to me;
his few good lines are such a shock I laugh; I also
find I get upset whenever worthy Homer dozes off,
but into works that long a little sleep must steal.   360
Poems are like pictures: the closer you stand to one,
the better it holds you; another gains as you withdraw.
This one loves shadow, this likes being seen in light
and fears no critic's wit, no matter how well honed.
One pleases once, one always will, though seen ten times.   365

Older brother, though you've learned from your father
and have wisdom of your own, let me offer you these words
to keep in mind: in some fields "average" will suffice,
there's no disputing that. A legal adviser and attorney
of moderate skill, not a great speaker like Messalla   370
and not in Aulus Cascellius's class for learning,
can still be useful. But poets of moderate skill
neither gods nor men endure; neither do publishers.
At a generally good dinner, inharmonious table music,
heavy ointments, and bitter honey on the poppy seeds   375
are most offensive, since no dinner has to have them,
and a poem, something born and meant to please the mind,
that falls a bit below the top comes too near bottom.
A man who knows no sports won't touch its armory;
without training he lets discus, hoop, and spear alone   380
rather than be laughed at by a crowd no one would blame.
But a man who knows no poetry will dare to write. Why not?
He's free and freeborn; most importantly, he's rich,
rich enough to be a knight, and morally impeccable.
But you will do or say nothing Minerva[1] wouldn't like.   385
Make this your judgment, this your plan. So, if someday
you write a poem, give it to stern Maecius's ears,
and your father's and mine; then for nine years keep it
safely withindoors. Making changes is quite allowable,
before you publish. Once freed, words can't return.   390
The gods sent Orpheus to savage mankind in the woods
to stop their murdering and refine their barbarous food,
and so our legends say he tamed fierce lions and tigers;
the legends also say that Amphion, who founded Thebes,
upraised its stones with lyre music and with charming words   395
could place them where he wished. This was the old wisdom
which divided public from private, sacred from secular,
outlawed free coupling, made marriage rites for man and wife,
erected cities, and carved codes of law on wooden tablets.
Therefore fame and honor came to our inspired bards   400
and to their songs. Following them, noble Homer
and Tyrtaeus sent virile souls to Mars and battle,
rousing men with verse. Oracles were made in meter,
and life's road was carefully described. Lyric sought
respect from kings, and dramatic festivals arose to mark   405
the end of long, hard work. So, the skillful lyric Muse
and Apollo the singer need never make you feel ashamed.
Does nature make a poem worth praising or does art?
An old question. I don't see the purpose either of art
without raw talent or of genius unrefined; for each thing   410
seeks the other's help, and the two combine as friends.
A runner who really wants to finish first across the line
trained hard and suffered as a boy; he froze and sweated,

1. As the goddess of the intellectual powers; the phrase means something like "against the dictates of wisdom."

shunned wine and women. The contestant on the pipe
at Delphi[2] first learned his art and feared his teacher.   415
It's not enough to say, "I just gush gorgeous poems.
Losers? they stink. It would disgrace me to be passed
or to admit I just don't know an art I never learned."
Like a crowd that swarms around a spieling auctioneer,
yes men seeking bargains obey the summons of a poet   420
rich in land and rich in cash he loans at interest.
If, moreover, he can put a fancy dinner on the table,
deliver deadbeats and untie friends from legal knots
that pinch, it would amaze me if he ever learned,
the lucky stiff, to tell a real friend from a fake.   425
If you've given or if you plan to give a man a present,
don't bring your poetry to him, not when he's filled
with joy: of course he'll rave: "Lovely! Perfect! Great!"
He'll turn pale at the right places, even dribble tears
from sympathetic eyes; he'll jump up, stomp the ground.   430
Just as hired mourners at a funeral lament and carry on
with almost greater passion than those whose hearts are sad,
your phonies will seem more moved than givers of true praise.
We hear how kings will urge a man to drink repeated cups
and twist the truth with wine from anyone they probe,   435
eager to learn his value as a friend. If you write poems,
never be deceived by foxy souls who flatter subtly.
If you recited to Quintilius, he'd say, "Please change
this line and that." Should you say you couldn't do it,
after making two or three attempts in vain, he'd order you   440
to take those malformed lines and return them to the anvil.
If you preferred defending what was wrong to changing it,
not one more word or bit of useless help would he expend
to turn you from your matchless love of self and work.
A good man with good judgment is hard on flat, dull lines,   445
condemns those that are rough, marks each confusing phrase
with a black slash of his pen. He chops away at frills,
demands that light be shed on anything not clear,
points out ambiguities, notes what must be changed,
acts like Aristarchus, and never says, "Why irritate   450
my friend with little things?" Little things can ruin him
if they bring about one rude reception, one public sneer.
Like a frantic sufferer from severest mange or jaundice,
or the wild priestly dancers and those Diana's driven mad,
the crazy poet makes all fear his touch and run away,   455
all wise men, though reckless boys harass and follow him.
And if, while wandering, staring into space and burbling verses,
as intent on them as is a hunter on a bird, he tumbled down
inside a well or ditch, although his bellow carried far, "Help!
Romans, help!," no one there would want to pull him out.   460
If, however, someone did, and prepared to drop a line,
I would suggest, "Who knows he didn't *jump* down there,

2. Games were held at Delphi, seat of the famous oracle; they included musical competitions.

and would rather not be saved?" The Sicilian poet's fate
I'd then describe: desiring to be thought a deathless god,
ice-cold Empedocles took up a pose on Aetna's fiery brink   465
and dropped. Stand up for poets' rights and let them die.
Save a man against his will? That's just like killing him.
He's tried before; nor will he, if he's saved, now
be a man and lay aside this love he has for famous deaths.
It isn't clear what makes him go on writing; perhaps   470
he urinated on his father's ashes or by some scandal
befouled holy ground. He's surely mad and, like a bear
with strength enough to break the bars that keep him in,
the fierce reciter makes learned and unlearned run in fear.
Any victim that he grabs, he holds, and kills by reading,   475
for he never leaves the skin till filled with blood—a leech.

Glossary

Compiled by Mary Hackney

Accius Roman poet (170–ca. 85 B.C.) who adapted many themes of Greek tragedy to the Roman stage; his florid style invited parody.

Aeschylus The famous Athenian tragedian (525/4–456 B.C.), largely responsible for introducing impressive costume, the characteristic buskin, and stately dances to the drama.

Afranius Lucius Afranius, born 154 B.C.; the most prolific writer of *comoediae togatae*, comedies based on Italian domestic life.

Agave Legendary mother of King Pentheus of Thebes. Euripides' tragedy *The Bacchae* relates that she was driven mad by the god Dionysus and, along with the other Bacchantes, tore Pentheus apart. Unaware of her madness, she returned to town displaying her own son's head as a hunting trophy.

Agrippa M. Vipsanius Agrippa (64 or 63–12 B.C.), the influential friend and supporter of Augustus, to a great extent reponsible for the emperor's previous victories over Sextus Pompeius and Marc Antony. As aedile in 33 B.C., he spent his own wealth freely on public entertainments and urban beautification.

Alcinoos King of the Phaeacians, who received Odysseus hospitably and sent him back to Ithaca in one of his people's magic ships.

Amphion Son of Jupiter and Antiope, brother of Zethus; famous musician and builder of the walls of Thebes.

Ancus Ancus Martius, the fourth king of Rome (640–616 B.C.).

Antenor An old and venerable Trojan chief who proposed that Helen be restored to the Greeks.

Antiphates King of the cannibal Lestrygonians, whose followers devoured one of Odysseus' crew and, by throwing huge boulders, sank all the ships except the one which Odysseus captained. (*Odyssey* X.100 ff.)

Antony Marcus Antonius, the triumvir, who ruled the Roman world jointly with Octavian and Lepidus.

Apelles The famous Greek painter (fl. ca. 332 B.C.), who did portraits of Philip, Alexander, and their friends; also noted for doing a self-portrait and writing a book on the art of painting.

Apollo Son of Jupiter and Leto, brother of Diana; god of the sun, poetry, music, fine arts, medicine, and prophecy.

Appius Appius Claudius Pulcher, censor in 50 B.C., who purged from the senatorial lists the names of many nobles and of all freedmen's sons.

Arbuscula A well-known actress of Cicero's time.

Archilochus Archilochus of Paros, a seventh-century B.C. writer of vitriolic iambic poetry. Horace drew on his verse as a model for his own *Epodes*, much as he drew on Lucilius as a model for the *Satires*.

Aristarchus A Homeric critic (fl. 180 B.C.) of Alexandria, known for his rigorousness and severity.

Aristippus Founder of the hedonistic Cyrenaic school of philosophy, whose basic doctrine Horace states in *E.I.1.19*.

Aristius Fuscus One of Horace's most valued friends, addressed by the poet in *Odes* I.22 and *E*.I.10.

Arrius Q. Arrius, a contemporary of Cicero, known to have given a lavish funeral entertainment after his father's death.

Atta T. Quinctius Atta (died 78 B.C.), a writer of *comoediae togatae* and elegaic epigrams.

Augustus Title conferred upon Octavian (q.v.) by the Roman Senate in 27 B.C.

Aulus Cascellius See Cascellius.

Barrus A particularly sharp-tongued man.

Bellona A Roman war deity, the sister of Mars, whose rites were often celebrated with frenzied self-mutilation.

Bullatius A friend of Horace; otherwise unknown.

Cadmus Founder of Thebes; after the metamorphosis of his daughter Ino, he went into voluntary exile with his wife, Harmonia. When they arrived in Illyria, they were changed into serpents.

Caecilius Caecilius Statius (fl. 179 B.C.), a comic poet who wrote highly regarded *fabulae palliatae*, comedies which adapted the Greek New Comedy style.

Caesar A family name in the Julian clan. C. Julius Caesar, the famous dictator of Rome, left his gardens to the Roman people by will (*S*.I.9.18); his great-nephew and adopted son, C. Julius Caesar Octavianus, became the emperor Augustus. See Octavian, Augustus.

Callimachus The famous Alexandrian poet (ca. 305–ca. 240 B.C.), whose erudition, experimentation, and versatility of style made him an important influence on later Roman elegy.

Calvus Roman poet and orator of the generation before Horace's; a friend of Catullus.

Camilli The clan of M. Furius Camillus, the general who freed Rome from the Gauls in 390 B.C.; it embodied traditional Roman values.

Canidia A witch, whose character Horace may have based on that of some notorious contemporary figure.

Canusium City of the Italian region of Apulia, where both Greek and Latin were spoken.

Cascellius Aulus Cascellius, a noted orator and jurist of Cicero's time.

Cassius One of the slayers of Julius Caesar, called Cassius of Parma in *E*.I.4.3 to distinguish him from the better known leader of the plot, C. Cassius Longinus; Cassius of Parma was also a poet, identified by the scholiasts with the Cassius Etruscus of *S*.I.10.61.

Castor and Pollux Twin brothers, the sons of Leda and Zeus (who came to her in the form of a swan). Castor was known for his excellent horsemanship, Pollux for his skill in boxing; both joined the Argonauts in the quest for the Golden Fleece. When the brothers died they were placed in the heavens as the constellation Gemini.

Catius Speaker in *S*.II.4; his identity is uncertain.

Cato Marcus Porcius Cato the Censor (234–149 B.C.), famous for his stringent views on morality.

Catullus Lyric poet of the generation before Horace's.

Ceres The goddess of agriculture.

Cethegus An orator of early Republican Rome, consul in 204 B.C.

Charybdis A dangerous whirlpool in the Straits of Messina, opposite the lair of the sea monster Scylla (*Odyssey* XII.104 ff., 235 ff.).

Choerilus An epic poet from Iasos; wrote a poem of poor quality on the exploits of Alexander the Great, who rewarded the poet richly despite the poem's inferiority.

Chremes A character appearing in the comedies of Terence; the typical angry old man who scolds his son.

Chrysippus A Stoic philosopher, born in 280 B.C., who devoted his life to elaborating the Stoic system in numerous works. His writings became identified with Stoic orthodoxy, and often he, instead of Zeno, was spoken of as the founder of the school.

Cicuta A miserly moneylender.

Cinara A young woman briefly but nostalgically mentioned by Horace as a past lover (*E.*I.7.28, I.14.33; *Odes* IV.1.3, IV.13.21).

Cocceius L. Cocceius Nerva, great-grandfather of the emperor Nerva. In 40 B.C. he had helped to negotiate the treaty at Brundisium which had divided lands under Roman power among the triumvirs Antony, Octavian, and Lepidus. Consul in 36 B.C.

Crantor A philosopher of the Old Academy and prolific writer (ca. 335 B.C.–ca. 275 B.C.).

Craterus A well-known physician of Cicero's time.

Cratinus Writer of Greek Old Comedy (see *S.*I.4.1 and note).

Crispinus A verbose Stoic writer whom Horace despised.

Curii The clan of M. Curius Dentatus, consul in 290 B.C. and conqueror of Pyrrhus, who was considered an exemplar of old Roman virtue.

Cyclops One of the Cyclopes, a one-eyed race of giant herdsmen; usually the Cyclops Polyphemus, whom Odysseus blinded (*Odyssey* IX.105 ff.).

Dacians A people living on the north bank of the Danube River, who had allied themselves with Antony against Octavian prior to the Battle of Actium.

Decemvirs The board of ten magistrates who, in the fifth century B.C., composed the Twelve Tables, a compilation of fundamental Roman laws originating in ancient custom.

Demetrius A professional musician, one of Horace's detractors; probably the "Monkeyface" of *S.*I.10.18.

Democritus Philosopher (ca. 460–ca. 370 B.C.) from Abdera in Thrace, who adopted and refined his master Leucippus' theory that the ultimate principles of reality are atoms and void. He was supposedly so engrossed in his scientific speculations that he allowed his farm to go to ruin through mere neglect.

Diana Sister of Apollo, goddess of the moon, whose beams supposedly caused "lunacy."

Egeria A nymph of Latium who, according to legend, was the consort and adviser to King Numa of Rome.

Empedocles Philosopher (ca. 493–ca. 433 B.C.) of Acragas in Sicily; postulated the Four Elements (fire, air, water, and earth) and believed that existence is held in balance by the perpetual conflict between the forces of Love and Strife. A man of amazing diversity, he was also orator, statesman, mystical leader, and poet.

Ennius Epic and tragic poet (239–169 B.C.), often called the "father of Roman verse"; best known for his *Annales,* an epic about Roman history.

Epicharmus A Greek writer (540–450 B.C.) of "Sicilian Comedy," which often burlesqued mythological figures such as Hercules and Odysseus; the dialogue of his plays was noted for its facility.

Epicurus The famous Athenian philosopher (341–270 B.C.), founder of the Epicurean school. He advocated pleasure as the natural human aim and highest good, defining it as freedom from pain and trouble and the attainment of an independent and imperturbable state of mind. Later critics of this school often confused Epicurean pleasure with baser forms of enjoyment.

Eupolis A playwright of Greek Old Comedy. See S.I.4.1.

Eutrapelus P. Volumnius Eutrapelus, a Roman knight of Cicero's time and a friend of Antony. He received his cognomen on account of his ready wit (*eutrapelia*).

Evander Legendary king of Pallanteum, who, according to Vergil's *Aeneid,* welcomed Aeneas to his home on the Palatine Hill.

Fabius A boring Stoic writer.

Florus See Julius Florus.

Fonteius Capito A close friend and diplomatic agent of Antony; became consul in 33 B.C.

Fundanius Horace's friend, who describes the dinner party of Nasidienus in S.II.8; probably a writer of comedies. See S.I.10.42.

Fuscus See Aristius Fuscus.

Genius A guardian spirit possessed by every human being and ending its existence when he did.

Glycon Well-known athlete.

Gracchus The Gracchus brothers, Gaius and Tiberius, were famous orators and social reformers of second-century B.C. Rome; Gaius, the younger of the two, was especially esteemed for his rhetorical skill.

Helicon The mountain in Boeotia traditionally thought to be inhabited by the Muses.

Hercules Legendary Greek hero, the son of Jupiter and Alcmena, often worshipped as a patron god by gladiators (*E*.I.1.5) and sometimes, like Mercury, considered a god of gain (S.II.6.12).

Hermogenes See Tigellius.

Homer The famous Greek epic poet, to whom the *Iliad* and the *Odyssey* are attributed.

Iccius A friend of Horace, addressed in *Odes* I.29; otherwise unknown.

Ilia Mother of the twins Romulus and Remus, the legendary founders of Rome.

Ino Daughter of Cadmus, wife of Athamas. After her husband went insane and dismembered one of their sons, she fled with the remaining son; both were turned into sea deities—she into Leuconoe and he into Palaemon.

Io Daughter of Inachus; Jupiter lusted after her and therefore turned her into a heifer to avert Juno's suspicion. Juno ordered the hundred-eyed giant Argos to guard her, but Jupiter sent Hermes to kill the giant and set her free. Io then wandered over the world, constantly tormented by a gadfly sent by Juno, until she came to Egypt. There she was metamorphosed by Jupiter back into a woman and bore him a son named Epaphus.

Ixion King of the Lapiths, father of Pirithous; killed his father-in-law and later attempted to rape Juno. Zeus struck him with a thunderbolt and ordered Hermes to tie him to an endlessly revolving wheel in the underworld as punishment for his audacity.

Janus The double-faced god of beginnings and new undertakings and, therefore, of morning.

Julius Florus A friend of Horace and Tiberius who studied oratory and possibly wrote satires (*E*.I.3.1, *E*.II.2.1).

Juno Queen of the gods, wife of Jupiter. The basket-bearers in her religious processions walked with a slow and dignified stride.

Laelius C. Laelius Sapiens, friend of Scipio Aemilianus Africanus (q.v.) with whom he shared a considerable interest in literature and philosophy; consul in 140 B.C.

Lamia (1) L. Aelius Lamia, a good friend of Horace, addressed in *Odes* I.26 and mentioned in *Odes* III.17; consul in A.D. 3 (*E*.I.14.6); (2) a female bogy who supposedly devoured children (*A.P.* 340).

Lares Household gods; native Roman rather than Greek deities.

Laverna The goddess of thievery.

Liber Dionysus, the god of wine, who "liberates" the drinker; hence the adage *"in vino veritas"* (see *S*.I.4.89). He was considered, more seriously, as a civilizer of mankind who taught the art of growing vines (*E*.II.1.5.)

Libitina Roman goddess of death.

Livius Andronicus The earliest known Latin writer, whose production of a play at Rome in 240 B.C. was considered the formal beginning of Roman literary history; wrote tragedies, comedies, and a famous translation of the *Odyssey* into Saturnian verse.

Lollius (1) M. Lollius, consul in 21 B.C., to whom Horace addressed *Odes* IV.9 (*E*.I.20.28); (2) Lollius Maximus, perhaps a relative of the former, who had served as a soldier in the Cantabrian War (25–24 B.C.) in northern Spain (*E*.I.2.1., *E*.I.18.1).

Lucilius A writer of satires (180–103 B.C.), acknowledged by Horace, Persius, and Juvenal as the founder of the tradition of Roman satire. Lucilian satire was noted for attacking well-known contemporary figures by name.

Lucullus L. Licinius Lucullus, consul in 74 B.C., who received an extraordinary command to continue the war against Mithridates. After he returned to Rome in 63 B.C., his name became a byword for luxurious living.

Lynceus Keen-sighted Greek hero, one of the Argonauts who set out in search of the Golden Fleece.

Lysippus Famous sculptor from Sicyon (fl. ca. 328 B.C.). Because of the precision of his detail and his ability to capture his model's momentary appearance, he alone was allowed to sculpt Alexander the Great.

Maecenas A Roman knight from an ancient Etruscan family. Though he never held public office, as the trusted friend of Augustus he served as counselor on home affairs and diplomatic agent. An aesthete and patron of letters, he befriended and included in his artistic circle Horace, Vergil, and Propertius, among others.

Maecius See Tarpa.

Mars Son of Jupiter and Juno; the god of war.

Medea The famous mythical sorceress, daughter of Colchian Aeetes. She fled with Jason after helping him obtain the Golden Fleece; when he later deserted her for another woman, she killed their common children. The subject of a tragedy by Euripides.

Menander The famous playwright (342–ca. 290 B.C.) of Greek New Comedy.

Mercury Messenger of the gods and patron god of gain and commerce.

Messalla Name associated with Roman family which included M. Valerius Messalla Corvinus (S.I.10.29, 85).

Metella Probably Cornelia Metella, the dissolute wife of P. Cornelius Lentulus Spinther, a contemporary of Cicero.

Midas Mythical king who turned all he touched to gold until relieved of this gift by bathing in the Pactolus, which acquired it.

Mimnermus A sixth-century B.C. elegiac poet from Colophon, whose musical verse displays playful eroticism and a love of pleasure.

Mount Alba A mountain near Rome, considered especially sacred in early Roman worship; the closest Roman analogue to the Greek Mt. Helicon, home of the Muses.

Mucius A well-known jurist, probably either P. Mucius Scaevola (consul in 133 B.C.) or Q. Mucius Scaevola (consul in 95 B.C.).

Musa Antonius Musa, freedman physician who introduced the cold water cure in 23 B.C.; Augustus was one of his patients.

Naevius (1) A spendthrift (S.I.1.101); a man lax about running his household (S.II.2.68), perhaps a different person from the first reference. (2) Poet from Campania (E.II.1.53) who wrote tragedies, comedies, and an epic, the *Bellum Poenicum*, in Saturnian verse; was first to produce *fabulae praetextae*, original tragedies based on Roman material. Died 204 B.C.

Nerius A moneylender or, perhaps, an agent who drew up loan contracts.

Nestor King of Pylos, the eldest Greek to sail against the Trojans; a respected but somewhat ineffectual counselor.

Nomentanus A spendthrift (S.I.1.102; S.I.8.11; S.II.1.22; S.II.3.175, 224), a parasite (S.II.8.23, 25, 60), perhaps a different person from the previous references.

Numa Numa Pompilius, the second king of Rome; supposed ancestor of Pisos (A.P. 292).

Numicus Addressed in E.I.6; otherwise unknown.

Octavian The future emperor Augustus. Though only the great-nephew of Julius Caesar by blood, he was adopted by the dictator as son and heir. Also referred to as Caesar and Augustus (q.v.).

Octavius Octavius Musa, an historian and poet.

Orcus The god of the underworld; synonymous with death.

Orpheus Mythical Thracian bard whose playing charmed even wild beasts.

Osiris An Egyptian god, the husband of Isis.

Pacuvius Born 220 B.C. in Brundisium; a famous writer of tragedies, the nephew and literary successor of Ennius.

Paulus Name associated with a distinguished Roman family which included Scipio Africanus (q.v.)

Pausias A famous Greek painter of the fourth century B.C., master of the encaustic technique, a method of painting on wood or stone with hot wax as a medium for applying various colors.

Peleus The son of Aeacus, driven from Aegina because he murdered his half-brother Phocis; the subject of a tragedy by Sophocles.

Penelope The faithful wife of Ulysses. She resisted the suitors, who wasted her husband's goods while courting her.

Philippus L. Marcus Philippus, consul in 91 B.C., a distinguished lawyer known for his drive and wit.

Philodemus A poet and Epicurean philosopher who lived at Rome in the time of Cicero. *The Greek Anthology* includes several of his epigrams, but not the one referred to in S.I.2.121.

Phraates Parthian king who restored to Augustus in 20–19 B.C. the Roman standards taken from Crassus at the Battle of Carrhae.

Pindar The greatest of the Greek lyric poets, born 518 B.C. in Boeotian Cynocephelae. The choral *epinicia*, odes written in honor of victors at athletic festivals, are his only poems preserved today in better than fragmentary condition.

Plato The great Greek philosopher, pupil of Socrates. The Plato of S.II.3.11 is either the philosopher or a Greek comic poet of the same name.

Plautus The famous Roman comic poet (died ca. 184 B.C.); though considered a writer of *fabulae palliatae*, comedies in which the actors wore the Greek *pallium*, he often introduced material of his own invention and thus injected Roman material into Greek scenes.

Plotius A friend of Vergil and Horace; with L. Varius Rufus edited the *Aeneid* after Vergil's death.

Polemon A young Athenian man-about-town who happened, while returning from a party, to overhear Xenocrates lecturing on temperance. He was immediately converted and eventually became Xenocrates' successor as head of the Academy in 314 or 313 B.C.

Pollux See Castor.

Pompeius Grosphus A Roman knight and friend of Horace who owned a large estate in Sicily; addressed by Horace in *Odes* II.16.

Priam King of Troy during the famed Trojan War.

Priapus A fertility god, often depicted as a misshapen little man with oversized genitals. His statue was placed in gardens as a guardian deity and as a scarecrow to frighten away birds and thieves.

Procne Daughter of Pandion, king of Athens. Her husband Tereus raped her sister Philomela and then cut out the sister's tongue. Philomela wove a tapestry depicting the outrage and sent it to Procne, whereupon both sisters plotted revenge. They cut up and cooked the body of Procne's and Tereus' young son and served it up as food to the father. The gods then metamorphosed them all into birds: Tereus into a hoopoe or hawk, Philomela into a nightingale, and Procne into a swallow.

Proserpina Queen of the underworld, wife of Pluto.

Proteus A sea-god able to change himself into many different forms and therefore difficult to capture.

Pupius A writer of tragedies.

Pythagoras A sixth-century B.C. philospher, born in Greece, who emigrated to Croton in Italy and there founded a religious society. He and his followers believed in the immortality and transmigration of the human soul. Membership in the Pythagorean society entailed silence, self-examination, and abstention from certain foods, such as meat.

Quinctius Possibly the Quinctius Hirpinus to whom Horace addressed *Odes* II.11; otherwise unknown.

Quintilius Quintilius Varus, a friend of Vergil and Horace whose death is mourned by Horace in *Odes* I.24.

Quintus Arrius See Arrius.

Quirinus The deified Romulus, as representative of the Roman people.

Romulus Son of the god Mars and Rhea Silvia; twin brother of Remus; the mythical founder of Rome, worshipped as a god.

Roscius (1) A person otherwise unknown (S.II.6.35); (2) Quintus Roscius Gallus, the famous actor (*E.* II.1.82), was unrivaled in comedy but played tragic parts as well; a friend of Cicero, defended by the orator in a private suit (*pro Roscio*).

Scipio Scipio Aemilianus Africanus (ca. 184–129 B.C.), L. Aemilius Paulus' son, later adopted by the son of Scipio Africanus the Elder. For nearly twenty years a key figure in Roman politics, he is perhaps best known for the final overthrow of Carthage in 146 B.C. Along with his friends Laelius, Furius Philus, and others, he shared a philhellenic perspective and an interest in philosophy and literature; his support and friendship were important to the satirical poet Lucilius.

Scylla A monster dwelling on one side of the Straits of Messina, who snatched and devoured six of Odysseus' crew with her six heads as his ship sailed past (*Odyssey* XII.85 ff., 235 ff.).

Septimius Probably identical with the friend Horace addressed in *Odes* II.6.

Silvanus Italian god of gardens, forests, and boundaries.

Sisenna A sharp-tongued individual.

Sisyphus (1) Legendary founder of Corinth, famous for its exquisite bronze work (*S.*II.3.21). (2) A pet dwarf of Antony's (*S.*I.3.46).

Socrates The famous Athenian philosopher (469–399 B.C.) immortalized in Plato's dialogues; known for his relentless inquiry into questions of morality and the right conduct of life.

Sophocles The famous Greek tragic poet (ca. 496–406 B.C.); credited by Aristotle for introducing a third actor, instituting scene-painting, and enlarging the tragic chorus from twelve to fifteen.

Sosii The Sosii brothers, Roman booksellers who marketed Horace's works.

Stertinius A contemporary of Horace who wrote 220 volumes of Stoic precepts in Latin verse.

Suadela A goddess, the personification of persuasiveness.

Tantalus A legendary king, condemned to be punished eternally with hunger and thirst for dishonoring the hospitality of the gods.

Tarpa Spurius Maecius Tarpa, appointed by Pompey to decide what plays should be performed in the theater; referred to with respect in *A.P.* 387.

Tarquin Tarquinius Superbus, the last king of Rome, driven out in 510 B.C.

Telephus Son of Hercules and Auge; king of Mysia; was wounded by Achilles' spear and could only be cured by touching it again. His efforts to do this were the subject of a tragedy by Euripides.

Tellus The Roman goddess of Earth.

Terence Roman comic poet (185–159 B.C.). His play *Heautontimoroumenos*, or *The Self-punished Man*, portrays a father, stricken with remorse for his cruelty toward his son, who deprives himself of all comforts until the son returns home.

Thespis The traditional founder of tragedy; won the prize when tragedy was first performed at the Athenian Dionysia, sometime between 535 and 533 B.C.; was first to have an actor deliver prologues and converse with the chorus leader.

Tibullus Albius Tibullus (ca. 48–19 B.C.), the elegiac poet; temperamentally, he was somewhat sensitive and brooding. His verse dealt largely with love and longing for an idyllic life in the country.

Tigellius A well-known musician of Cicero's time (S.I.2.3; S.I.3.4). Hermogenes Tigellius is probably a separate person, a contemporary singer and poet whom Horace despised (S.I.3.129; S.I.4.72; S.I.9.25; S.I.10.18, 80, 90).

Torquatus Presumably one of the wealthy family of the Manlii Torquati; a busy lawyer and friend of Horace; probably the same person to whom Horace addressed *Odes* IV.7.

Trebatius C. Trebatius Testa, a distinguished lawyer who enjoyed the esteem of Cicero, Julius Caesar, and Augustus. His humorous disposition and advanced age made him ideal for the mock-legal consultation of S.II.1

Tullius Servius Tullius (578–535 B.C.); born a slave, he became the sixth king of Rome.

Turbo A small but courageous gladiator.

Tyrtaeus Greek elegiac poet (seventh century B.C.) who wrote war songs for the Spartans during the Second Messenian War.

Vala Numonius Vala, a friend of Horace; otherwise unknown.

Valgius C. Valgius Rufus, an elegiac poet to whom Horace addressed *Odes* II.9; became consul in 12 B.C.

Varius A tragic and epic poet; the friend of Vergil and Horace who introduced Horace to Maecenas.

Vergil The great poet Vergil, author of the *Eclogues* at this time, destined to write the *Georgics* and the *Aeneid*.

Vertumnus The old Italian god of the changing year and, thus, of all change.

Viscus One of the two sons of Vibius Viscus, a Roman knight. The brothers were both literary figures and friends of Horace and Maecenas; in S.I.10.83 Horace mentions them among the people whose approval he values.

Volteius Mena The name indicates that he was a freedman of Greek birth, whose former master and patron was named Volteius.